GAMING IN LICENSED PREMISES

A PRACTICAL GUIDE TO THE IMPACT AND
EFFECT OF THE GAMBLING ACT 2005

ON ALCOHOL-LICENSED PREMISES & CLUBS
IN ENGLAND AND WALES

If you would like to order a further copy please email
info@tavernapublishing.co.uk

First Published in Great Britain in 2009

Taverna Publishing is the publisher of Gaming in Licensed Premises.

Taverna Publishing,
PO Box 9888,
Newark,
NG24 9HN

ISBN : 978-0-9564129-0-4

CHANDLER®
BOOK DESIGN

Typeset in Gill Sans 10pt
by Chandler Book Design
www.chandlerbookdesign.co.uk

Printed in Great Britain by the
MPG Books Group,
Bodmin and King's Lynn

GAMING IN LICENSED PREMISES

Whur, Patrick, Woods, Andrew
and McGowan, Stephen J.

Taverna Publishing
P.O.Box 9888
Newark
NG24 9HN
2009

ABOUT THE AUTHORS

Patrick Whur

Paddy joined Walker Morris in April 2006 as a partner. Previously he was a partner at Poppleston Allen. Paddy has built a nationally acclaimed profile as a specialist in liquor, betting and gaming law. Praised for providing "a feasible idea of what you will achieve, rather than tell you what you want to hear", and ranked number 1 in the North East in Chambers Directory.

He represents national and international bookmakers and is playing a key role in the legal development of betting on the Internet. Over recent years he has represented; Ladbrokes, Betfred, The Tote, Coral, National Leisure, Mecca Bingo and a host of independents for Gambling Act advice.

Paddy was the lead lawyer in advising the Cyprus Government on Betting & Gaming Law. Undertaking a review of their legislation. He was a contributor to Paterson's Licensing Acts on the Gambling Act 2005 and is a regular speaker at industry events.

Paddy is a Solicitor-Advocate (Higher Courts all Proceedings) having attained his higher rights of audience from the Solicitors Regulation Authority. This effectively allows him to act as advocate representing clients in all criminal and civil courts in the UK. He is also a visiting lecturer at Warwick University having written the Gambling Course for the Certificate of Higher Education in Licensing Law.

Andrew Woods

Andrew joined Walker Morris as a partner in April 2006 having been a partner at Gosschalks and Poppleston Allen, bringing with him many years experience in licensing, betting and gaming. Andrew is highlighted in recent editions of the Chambers Guide to the Legal Profession, ranked as joint No1 in the North East, and quoted as being "top of the pile".

Andrew has represented a range of major betting, gaming and liquor clients including William Hill, Ladbrokes, Corals, The Barracuda Group, Novus Leisure, Thistle Hotels, TCG and the Spirit Group over his many years experience.

Andrew represented Clermont Leisure who made 30 applications for casino licences under the Gaming Act 1968 throughout the United Kingdom. He often conducted the advocacy himself and also was responsible for representing Clermont Leisure in the leading casino case of TC Projects which was decided by the Court of Appeal in April 2008.

Andrew has also advised a number of clients on establishing competitions on the Internet and other clients in creating gaming websites. He has also been instructed by Humberside Police in bringing review proceedings against holders of premises licences.

Andrew is a Solicitor-Advocate representing clients (Higher Courts all Proceedings) having attained his higher rights of audience from the Solicitors Regulation Authority allowing him to represent clients in all UK courts. He is a regular speaker at conferences and his articles have appeared in many legal journals.

Stephen J McGowan

Stephen works in the Hospitality & Leisure department of Scottish commercial law firm Tods Murray LLP (www.todsmurray.com). He is the author of "Gaming in Pubs & Clubs: The New Law" (2008), a Scottish guide to the new gambling laws, and the author of "Licensing and Gambling Law in Scotland: A Practical Guide" (2009).

Stephen is an Affiliate of the British Institute of Innkeepers, and is authorised to provide the Scottish Certificate for Personal Licence Holders and mandatory staff training. He is also the tutor for Central Law Training's paralegal certificate in licensing law, authored the course book, and lectures at Strathclyde University. Stephen was described in The Firm legal magazine as "every inch the renaissance legal professional" and won the prestigious Chairman's Award at the Law Awards 2008 for his contributions to licensing and gambling law in Scotland. Before going into private practice, Stephen worked for the Glasgow Licensing Board, and in the licensed trade itself as a bartender. He is a Member of the Institute of Licensing.

Stephen has acted for a wide variety of licensing and gambling clients from sole traders to national chains and has contributed dozens of articles to the trade press such as On Trade Scotland, The Publican, The Caterer, Scottish Licensed Trade News, and legal journal Scottish Licensing Law & Practice (www.sllp.co.uk).

TABLE OF CONTENTS

FOREWORD

The Licensing Act 2003 and Gambling Act 2005 introduced major regulatory reforms in the areas of alcohol, entertainment and late night refreshment, and gaming, betting and lotteries, respectively to replace previous legislation, much of it dating back to the 1960s. The changing nature of the leisure and gambling industries, along with technological changes, have transformed the social scene that the previous legislative provisions were seeking to regulate and the new legislation implements a modern system of licensing suitable for the 21st century.

A number of books have been written on the Licensing Act 2003 and Gambling Act 2005 explaining and analysing the new law. Each piece of legislation is detailed, extending to over 200 sections and several schedules, and is supplemented by both a tranche of secondary legislation and statutory guidance. Because of the breadth of coverage required, books on the two Acts have not been able to give the topic of gaming in licensed premises like public houses and clubs the detailed attention that it deserves.

The strength of this work is that its focus is specifically on this topic and the book will be a welcome addition to complement existing works on the Licensing Act 2003 and Gambling Act 2005. A more detailed analysis and exposition of gaming in licensed premises is provided than will be encountered in more general works on these two areas of licensing control and the authors specialist knowledge in the fields of alcohol and gambling licensing is evident throughout the text as the reader is guided through an area which has its fair share of difficulties and complexities.

The book should prove to be a valuable guide for those whose work includes gaming in licensed premises. This will most obviously include licensing practitioners, applicants and licensing authorities, but might also extend to others working in the field such as police licensing officers and training course providers. All should be able to obtain an enhanced understanding of gaming in licensed premises from this book.

Professor Colin Manchester
Professor of Licensing Law
University of Warwick
July 2009

ACKNOWLEDGEMENTS

The authors would like to thank the following people for their assistance:

Jonathan Hyldon for his overall contribution and his lead role in respect of certain chapters within the book, William Woods for his design and art work and Tracey Leavesley for the many hours spent typing.

In the usual way, we take responsibility for the finished work.

October 2009

PW and AW, Leeds
SJM, Edinburgh

CHAPTER ONE
INTRODUCTION

A BRAVE NEW WORLD

The Gambling Act 2005 came into force, in full, on 1 September 2007, as the ancien régime of gambling legislation crumbled away. At this time, licensing lawyers, licensing authorities and staff, magistrates courts, police and of course the trade all over the country were still finding their feet with the Licensing Act 2003 and its ramifications on liquor and entertainment licensing. In such a budding cauldron of provisions, consultations, regulations, Commissions, licensing authorities, Acts, Statutory Instruments and so forth, it is not surprising that the new gambling provisions – and how they impact on alcohol licensing – may not have been given the attention they deserve.

The purpose behind this book is to provide licensing lawyers and paralegals, licensing practitioners, licensing authorities, their legal officers and staff, police licensing officers, licensing course providers and trainers, and of course the licensed trade, with an easy to understand guide to gambling law, with a particular emphasis on how it affects premises licensed under the Licensing Act 2003, where the provision of alcohol is the main activity . Such a guide has become necessary, it seems, because in recent years, gambling law has suffered with its status of alcohol licensing's neglected (and difficult) little brother. As a result this complex area is often overlooked.

This is not clarified by the introduction of fresh legislation, as the Gambling Act 2005 is filled with a myriad of bamboozling provisions. This text should not be used by itself as a guide to the Act. In all matters we would refer the reader to the text of the Act, guidance documents and the Gambling Commission website.

The law regulating gambling in the UK was, until 1 September 2007, spread across a variety of archaic pieces of legislation but principally found in three Acts: the Gaming Act 1968, the Lotteries and Amusements Act 1976, and the Betting, Gaming and Lotteries Act 1963 . This triumvirate held sway for decades and, insofar as their aim was to prevent criminal elements from entering gambling, they were generally viewed as successful. However, advances in technology and a more fundamental acceptance of gambling in society had resulted in them becoming more and more redundant, and ultimately led to the need for an overhaul. It is worthwhile to quickly remind ourselves of the general features of this now obsolete legislation, in order to set the scene.

THE GAMING ACT 1968

The Gaming Act 1968 was principally borne out of a belief that gambling was an inherently dubious and regrettable pastime; indeed, it can be viewed as a sort of grudging tolerance of society's penchant for the thrill of chance . The majority of the people in the world of liquor licensing dipped their toes in the provisions of the Act by applying for permits to operate Amusements with Prizes (otherwise known as "fruit machines") under s.34(1) or (5E) of the 1968 Act; but on an odd occasion the 1968 Act would need to be dusted down to look at a special type of permit under s.6, which could be used, it was argued, to facilitate gambling of other nature on alcohol-licensed premises. The Act's main practical purpose came from regulating casinos, bingo halls, race tracks and machine gaming.

The legislation of the 1960s was set against a backdrop of illegal casinos, back street bookies and illegal street betting and gaming. The tenor of the legislation was that permission for commercial gambling was a privilege and not a right. The law created a restrictive environment where facilities were strictly controlled so as not to encourage people to dwell on licensed premises. Another aim was to attempt to outlaw strong-arm tactics relating to the supply of gaming machines in licensed premises.

THE LOTTERIES AND AMUSEMENTS ACT 1976

Applications under s.5 of the 1976 Act would be dealt with by the local authority for the area in which the lottery was to be held and registered, for an initial fee of £35.00 and an annual renewal of £17.50 thereafter. Registration under this Act allowed lotteries to be held so long as the ticket price did not exceed £1, full details of the charity, promoter, relevant council/local authority and other information had to be contained on the face of the ticket and the total value of the tickets could not exceed £20,000. Licensing practitioners generally came across this procedure when clients such as sports clubs operated internal lotteries for their members.

THE BETTING, GAMING AND LOTTERIES ACT 1963

This Act provided regulation for pool promoter's registration, bookmaker's permits and betting office licences.

Pool betting is where the stakes paid by participants are collated and, after deduction of expenses, the total is shared amongst winners depending on the outcome. The best-known example of this type of gambling is of course pool betting based on the outcome of football results, "The Pools". In order to promote a pool, registration was sought under this Act through an appropriate council at an initial cost of £450.00 with an annual renewal of £300.00 thereafter.

Bookmaker's permits and betting office licences under this Act were dealt with by the Magistrates' Courts. Applicants for a bookmaker's permit could apply to any Magistrates' Court in England and Wales as long as they had a geographical link, for example, their ordinary place of residence or registered office of their company. Once granted the permit would last for three years and a renewal would need to be lodged roughly five weeks in advance.

This led to internet operators applying for permits at the Magistrates' Court covering their where their solicitors' or accountants' offices were situated. There were growing concerns that the entry level was too low and regulation sparse.

Betting office licences also had a three year duration, most of which fell for renewal in March each year. Criteria for refusal of these included: that the applicant was not a fit and proper person; that the premises were not suitable; or that there was no unmet demand. "Demand" for betting facilities in a certain area could be calculated by figures gained from the betting shop. The fact that each betting transaction has to be recorded on a numbered betting slip, for duty collection purposes, led to a system of "slip checking", which in turn allowed for a potential new operator to place a bet on each of the tills on a weekly basis at existing betting shops and accurately assess a number of betting slips transacted in the shop. This would provide an accurate estimate of the demand for betting when judged against averaged figures.

These three statutory regimes ultimately proved to be unworkable with the increasing advances of technology in gaming and their death knell was sounded when Sir Alan Budd reported his 260 page report with no fewer than 175 recommendations detailing his findings as to the Gambling Industry and its regulation in July 2001. This report began the process that led to the Gambling Act 2005.

CHAPTER TWO THE GAMBLING ACT 2005 – AN OVERVIEW

ORIGIN OF THE ACT

The Gambling Act 2005 started life as a government white paper entitled "A Safe Bet for Success"[1] which itself was a response to "The Gambling Review Report" ("the Budd Report")[2] the report by the Gambling Review Body published in July 2001 chaired by Sir Alan Budd. "A Safe Bet for Success" resulted in a draft bill published in November 2003, which was later amended in February and March of 2004 before eventually reaching the statute books. At the time this legislation was progressing through Parliament[3] there was a significant national media outcry, with banner headlines warning Britain was heading for ruin, would become a Las Vegas style island, much of this being promoted and funded by interested parties who saw the potential harm to their vested interests.

The Secretary of State for the Department of Culture, Media and Sport (DCMS) at the time was Tessa Jowell, and she was forced to defend the legislation through a difficult passage. The headlines generated by such debate perpetuated into the Gordon Brown administration, and in February 2008 a very public climb-down from the award of a super casino

---

1 CM.5397.

2 Cm.5206. See further Ferrie, A. (2001) "Budd Report paves way for major gaming changes" 20 SLLP 7.

3 Due to its considerable pace, many MPs were put out by the lack of debating time set aside and the haste with which it was passed was generally a source of irritation.

in Manchester was announced[4]. Indeed, much of the press attention on the Act has been about super casinos and problem gambling. The reality for licensing practitioners is much more elaborate (and less sensational), as the Gambling Act does not merely regulate casinos – although going by the press you would be forgiven for thinking that was the case. The Act was published on 7 April 2005 and came fully into force on 1 September 2007.

The Gambling Act 2005 now regulates all forms of gambling in the UK with the exception of the National Lottery[5] and spread betting[6].

THE LICENSING OBJECTIVES

In the introduction to his report, Sir Alan Budd said "*I hope we shall be able to establish principles which are acceptable to all sensible people and shall make proposals consistent with those principles*"[7]. This hope has become a reality, as it resulted in Section 1 of the Act laying down three "guiding objectives", which are:

- Preventing gambling from being a source of crime or disorder, being associated with crime or disorder or being used to support crime
- Ensuring that gambling is conducted in a fair and open way
- Protecting children and other vulnerable persons from being harmed or exploited by gambling

As with the equivalent objectives in the Licensing Act 2003 and the Licensing (Scotland) Act 2005 , these objectives constitute the foundation

---

4 Andy Burnham, then Culture Secretary, said of this that there was "no consensus" that such a super casino would have a potentially negative impact.

5 The National Lottery continues to be regulated by The National Lottery etc Act 1993.

6 Spread betting is controlled by the Financial Services Authority as it constitutes a contract under s.412 of The Financial Services & Markets Act 2000 – see s.10 of the 2005 Act.

7 Cm.5206, Introduction.

for how the purpose of the Act is to be interpreted, and act as a guide for decisions made by those authorities who consider applications or other matters resulting from its incorporation into UK law. An "unwritten" fifth objective, of sorts, is to take account of ever advancing technology and how that has manifested in forms of gambling.

OPERATING LICENCES, PREMISES LICENCES & PERSONAL LICENCES

Another similarity with the Licensing Act 2003 and Licensing (Scotland) Act 2005 is the creation of "personal" and "premises" licences, although here there is an additional permission known as an "operating licence" which is a precedential condition required to allow gambling to take place. This proliferation of the use of the word "licence" has led to premises holding such permissions issued under the Licensing Act 2003 and the Licensing (Scotland) Act 2005 being termed as "alcohol-licensed premises" by Westminster and Holyrood, to afford assistance in differentiation. We have applied the principle in this text also. For the purposes of brevity we have, on the whole, refrained from discussing the procedural aspects of personal and premises licences under the 2005 Act and the reader is advised, as is the case elsewhere in the text, to refer to the Act if further clarification is sought.

OPERATING LICENCES

Operating licences are introduced under Part 5 of the Act and represent a key aspect of control over gambling in the UK. They are issued by the Gambling Commission to persons/corporate bodies wishing to offer gambling services in respect of specific types of gambling and the applicant has to satisfy a gruelling series of tests largely designed to prove that he is of fit and proper character. S.65 of the Act lists the types of operating licence available:

- a casino operating licence
- a bingo operating licence
- a general betting operating licence
- a pool betting operating licence
- a betting intermediary operating licence
- a gaming machine general operating licence for an adult gaming centre
- a gaming machine general operating licence for a family entertainment centre
- a gaming machine technical operating licence
- a gambling software operating licence
- a lottery operating licence

There are a few circumstances where there is a crossover between alcohol and entertainment licensing and Gambling Act licensing, for example with bowling alleys which can also be classed as "family entertainment centres" (FECs); the grey area over what is meant by a "lottery" in respect of the final type of operating licence noted above; providing facilities for remote gaming; and high level bingo. We will discuss these in detail later in this book. The last date for an existing operator to lodge an application for an operating licence with continuation rights was 27 April 2007. This created a flurry of activity as existing operators rushed to complete lengthy application forms to ensure that they did not lose the ability to continue to operate at the end of the transitional period, such continuation rights allowing continued commercial activity pending the outcome of their application for an Operating Licence. This did not confer grandfather rights but it allowed continuation until the substantive application had been determined.
This also led to a number of old, smaller operators either selling their businesses or giving up due to them not having the desire to go through such a detailed application and period of change.

The holder of an operating licence may go on to establish premises to provide the relevant gambling facilities, however it is very common for the operating licence to have a condition limiting the number of premises which may be operated.

PREMISES LICENCES

Not to be confused with premises licences under the Licensing Act 2003 or the Licensing (Scotland) Act 2005, this type of licence is required to offer gambling facilities for casinos, bingos, betting premises (including tracks), adult gaming centres and family entertainment centres and, put simply, authorises the relevant form of gambling to take place on the premises specified in the licence. Crucially, an applicant for a premises licence must first be the holder of an operating licence. Once granted the licence has no expiry date, although an annual fee must be paid[8],, it is capable of being transferred[9], and there is provision for review[10]. Applications for premises licences are made to the relevant licensing authority, and as a result the form, content and regulations for premises licences are controlled by Government[11].

Section 154 of the Act deals with delegation of consideration of premises licences in England and Wales. The licensing authority may delegate the consideration of such applications to the clerk or his assistants. This avoids the necessity of holding a meeting to consider a premises licence application as the licence is granted as requested if there are no

---

8 s.184.

9 s.188.

10 s.200.

11 There are separate regulations for premises licences procedures in England & Wales and in Scotland, primarily because the body charged with processing such applications is the local authority (council) in England & Wales, whereas in Scotland it is the separate licensing boards constituted under the Licensing (Scotland) Act 2005 which process gambling premises licences.

representations. This delegated power does not apply where there have been relevant "representations" made to the application[12].

There is a provision for the imposition of mandatory, default and local conditions[13]; a premises licence may not be issued subject to a condition requiring membership for some or all parts of the premises[14], a duty is placed on the licensing authority to maintain a register[15], no gambling facilities can be made available on Christmas Day[16], and the licensing authorities cannot have regard to whether the proposal is likely to be in accordance with planning permission and building regulations, in much the same way that a planning committee cannot give consideration as to whether a premises is likely to be granted an alcohol licence[17]. There is provision for review of premises licences in order to maintain control of their operation, which may be instigated by a responsible authority or interested party[18], or by the licensing authority[19].

PERSONAL LICENCES

As with the equivalent provisions in the Licensing Act 2003, this type of licence is used for persons in a position of authority or management who work on gambling premises or offer gambling services remotely. The gambling personal licence is however, more of a badge of personal good character and integrity, as opposed to a symbol of training in the licensed trade. Unlike under the Licensing Act 2003 where a Personal Licence has a lifespan of ten years, a gambling Personal Licence is of indefinite

---

12 s.154(4).
13 ss.167 – 169. A Licensing Authority may not alter the mandatory conditions, but does have the power to amend or exclude default conditions.
14 s. 170.
15 s. 156.
16 s. 183.
17 s. 210.
18 S. 197.
19 S.200.

duration (subject to surrender, revocation etc). Applications for personal licences are made to the Gambling Commission.

There are two types of personal licence under the Act: the Personal Management Licence (PML) and the Personal Functional Licence (PFL). Section 127 makes a distinction between persons performing functions in a "management office", or persons performing a specific "operational function". The terms are defined under s.80 of the Act.

"**Management Office**" is defined in terms of the type of legal person holding the operating licence. The word "Office" is used in terms of a position held by an individual, rather than a business premises. The Act specifies the position to be held by persons holding personal licences, as follows:

- Limited Company: director
- Partnership: partner
- Unincorporated Association: any office holder
- In any case: persons with responsibility for the conduct of a person who performs an operational function in connection with a licensed activity ; or involved in "facilitating or ensuring" compliance with the operating licence

The Gambling Commission's website further states: "*Those who are responsible for the following management functions...will require PML's*":

- overall strategy and delivery of gambling operations
- financial planning
- control and budgeting
- marketing and commercial development
- regulatory compliance
- gambling related IT provision and security

"**Operational Function**" means a function enabling a person to:

- influence the outcome of gambling
- receive or pay money in connection with gambling
- manufacture, supply, install, maintain, or repair a gaming machine

PFL's will therefore relate to casino dealers, croupiers, cashiers, pit bosses, and so on.

The broad basis for all of this is, of course, a safety valve to ensure that persons involved with providing gambling, from staff on the ground all the way up to high-level management, have been involved in an application process to authorise them and ensure that they meet the required standards.

All Operating Licences have a condition to ensure that at least one person holds a PML and at least one person holds a PFL[20].

This level of licensing gives the Gambling Commission a higher standard of control and ability to monitor who is certificated to hold key positions in the gambling industry.

CODES OF PRACTICE

A new creation of the Act is the introduction of statutory Codes of Practice, under s.24. These codes must be adhered to by anyone providing any form of gambling facility under the Act, including persons who operate premises with a relevant alcohol licence. The publication of the Codes is a task for the Gambling Commission. There are specific

20 There is an exemption under s.129 for "small scale operators" defined in The Gambling Act 2005 (Definition of Small-scale Operator) Regulations 2006 SI 3266 as operators where there are less than three qualifying positions.

codes for distinct forms of gambling, which we have discussed in the relevant chapters below.

The Commission issued a general guidance document entitled "Licence Conditions and Codes of Practice" in June 2007 which sets out the generic rules for all holders of operating licences. It was updated on 1 October 2008 and had its first supplement issued on 28 January 2009, in relation to primary gambling activity. As explained elsewhere, it is unlikely any alcohol-licensed premises (whose primary function is the sale of alcohol) will require an operating licence and so this general code is not discussed further here, but the document and supplementary information is available from the Gambling Commission website.

CHAPTER THREE THE REGULATORS OF THE NEW REGIME

THE GAMBLING COMMISSION

Prior to the 2005 Act, regulation of the gambling industry was piecemeal with organisations such as the Gaming Board, the Jockey Club, and the Magistrates Courts all playing a part in regulation. Part 2 of and Schedule 4 to the Act has removed any compliance and regulatory provisions from these organisations with the creation of a single regulatory body, the Gambling Commission[21]. One of the key changes brought about by the Act is to have one regulator for the whole of the gambling industry – a sea change from the previous legislation.

The Commission is based in Birmingham, and is Chaired by Brian Pomeroy CBE as of 1 January 2008, who replaced Peter Dean CBE, the former head of the Gaming Board. Upon his appointment, Mr Pomeroy said:

> "My priority will be to make sure that the gambling industry meets the tough new standards required by the Act. In doing so, the Commission should not hesitate to use its array of new powers and sanctions to ensure that gambling remains fair and crime free and that proper protections for children and vulnerable adults are put in place"

21 The Jockey Club website states "*Released from its regulatory duties, the Jockey Club is focusing on its commercial activities*". http://www.thejockeyclub.co.uk/doc.php.

This protection may yet be funded by an "addiction tax" on gambling operators. This idea, an extension of the so-called "polluter pays" polemic, has already taken root in relation to alcohol-licensed premises in the form of the "Alcohol Disorder Zone" regulations although no local authority has yet implemented an order declaring such a zone; and the mechanism for such a levy for gambling premises is there[22]. The Government has, so far, elected to allow the industry to self-regulate in this area, but there are signs that this may change.

Baroness Neuberger was appointed to chair a committee to probe a voluntary contribution to a gambling addiction tax. She has announced to the industry if there is no voluntary agreement then an enforced levy will be imposed. The Gambling Commission is not a supporter of the voluntary agreement and continues to press for an enforced levy.

The Gambling Commission's principal functions are:

- to promote the licensing objectives;
- to consider applications for operating licences;
- to consider applications for personal licences;
- to issue Codes of Practice;
- to provide guidance to local authorities;
- to ensure compliance with the provisions of the Act;
- to pursue and prosecute offences under the Act;
- to collaborate with other relevant organisations;
- and to provide advice to the Secretary of State on the incidence an nature of gambling and its impact

22 The Scottish Government has promulgated a tartan version of the ADZ, known as the "Social Responsibility Fee". This proposal has met with obvious opposition from the licensed trade. It is part of the new Criminal Justice and Licensing Bill in Scotland which had yet to be put before the Scottish Parliament at the time of writing.

The Gambling Commission has taken the lead with the way forward in the new gambling landscape. It has embraced the information highway, and has a huge amount of information available on their website and through periodical email alerts for interested parties. Further, they have provided licensing authorities with a substantial amount of guidance, not simply on the new laws, but even on the information exchange itself[23]. Licensing Authorities have a duty to provide the Commission with a large amount of information - for example, regulatory returns and information on the number of applications granted or refused within a specific period. The only criticism here is the amount of new information being constantly produced[24].

GAMBLING COMMISSION'S STATEMENT OF PRINCIPLES

Under s.23 of the 2005 Act the Commission was charged with producing a "statement of principles". This was first released in December 2006 and covers three key areas: general principles; licensing objectives; and provisions of the Act:

General Principles

The Commission has set out the following general principles:

- to regulate gambling in the public interest;
- regulate in a transparent, accountable, proportionate, consistent and targeted manner;
- regulation will be risk-based;
- assessment of risk is based on evidence and best practice;

---

23 Gambling Commission Publication "Advice to Licensing Authorities on Information Exchange with the Gambling Commission", 2nd Ed., December 2007.

24 The authors believe that it would be helpful if the Gambling Commission website could be made easier to navigate; and with clear marking of documents which have been superseded. A new version of the website was due to go "live" as this book was being finalised.

- consultation; and
- effective use of resources.

Licensing Objectives

It is the duty of the Commission to "pursue and have regard" to the licensing objectives. This includes tackling crime, especially crime in which gambling is an intrinsic element; prevention of crime by screening, control and pursuit of offences; ensuring the rules of gambling are fair and that licences are issued to those who are suitable to offer gambling services; and to provide guidance and clarification regarding children and access to gambling to prevent exploitation.

Provisions of the Act

This element of the statement of principles is about how the Commission will consider applications made to it under the Act;

- to ensure competence;
- to assess financial circumstances of applicants;
- to assess suitability of machines and other gambling equipment; and
- procedural aspects regarding hearings.

The Statement of Principles is available to view in full at the Gambling Commission's website, which is noted in Appendix B.

THE GAMBLING APPEALS TRIBUNAL

A decision made by the Gambling Commission may be appealed to the Gambling Appeals Tribunal (under Part 7 of the Act), another creation of the 2005 Act to deal with appealed decisions by the Commission in respect of applications for operating licences and personal licences. A decision in respect of a premises licence application (or review of such a licence) is made to the licensing authority and an appeal would proceed to the Magistrates' Court.

The applicant for an Operating Licence, or anyone who made a representation to the application, may appeal. An appeal must be lodged no later than one month after the decision (although the Tribunal has the power to accept late appeals). A decision of the Tribunal may be further appealed, on a point of law, to the High Court. Appeals to the High Court would be on a point of law judged against the famous "Wednesbury Principles"[25].

THE DEPARTMENT OF CULTURE, MEDIA AND SPORT

The government department dealing with gambling law is the Department of Culture, Media & Sport. The DCMS website says they are "*responsible for the policy and ensuring that the necessary legislation is passed by Parliament*". It contains a wealth of information about the Parliamentary history of the Act, as well as access to a number of guidance documents and, of course, links to the full text of the Act itself as well as any secondary legislation such as statutory instruments.

DCMS will, from time to time, ask the Commission to produce information and analysis on certain subjects of interest to the government. In July 2008 DCMS asked the Commission for a special report on the impact of high stake, high prize gaming machines on problem gamblers. The report was published in an open letter to DCMS on 30 June 2009[26].

---

25 These were laid down in Associated Provincial Picture Houses Ltd v Wednesbury Corporation [1948] 1 KB 223 and are: 1) that there was an error on a point of law; 2) that the decision was *ultra vires*, 3) that the decision was unreasonable because a) the tribunal took account of a matter which it should not have, b) the tribunal did not take account of a matter which it should, and c) it was not a decision which any reasonable tribunal would have made.

26 This report, and others, are available from the Gambling Commission's website.

CHAPTER FOUR
GAMING MACHINES ON ALCOHOL-LICENSED PREMISES

A gaming machine is defined under the 2005 Act as a machine which is designed or adapted for use by individuals to gamble (whether or not it can also be used for other purposes)[27].

Gaming machines are one of the most popular forms of gambling in the UK. The Gambling Commission estimates that, in 2008 there were approximately 260,000 gaming machines in the UK; and that 14% of the population play them. In 2006/07, 26% of all machines were located in pubs, and 6% of all machines were in clubs. Gaming machines have been around for some time now - there is case law on the control of the old "penny-in-the-slot" machine going back to the late 19th century. The popularity of such machines increased considerably in the early 1960s, when the legislation of the time, coupled with advances in technology, led to "an explosion of the availability"[28] of machines. Part of the political impetus for the Gaming Act 1968 was in fact an attempt to control the situation.

AMUSEMENTS WITH PRIZES UNDER THE 1968 ACT

As touched on earlier, the law here was based in s. 34 of the Gaming Act 1968, which allowed the use on alcohol-licensed premises of "Amusements

27 Section 235(1).
28 Barker, K. & Hamilton, D.J. (1993) "Betting, Gaming and Lotteries", Fourmat Publishing, London: Page 103.

with Prizes" machines[29], either via a s.34(1) permit, allowing "Non All-Cash" machines, or a s.35(5E) permit, allowing "All-Cash" machines. These definitions relate to a time when it was quite unremarkable to play a slot machine which would return a mixture of coins and tokens[30], leading to the term "Non All-Cash".

Such machines are probably no longer in use on alcohol-licensed premises but do retain a position in seaside fairs and premises of that nature. In contrast, the "All-Cash" machine is in reality the type of machine to be found in most pubs, nightclubs and so on and is a slot machine typically with a stake from 30p to £1 and, at the time of writing, up to a jackpot of £70. The stakes and prizes have increased almost three fold in the last year three years - from 25p and £25 to 50p and £35 on 27 October 2006, as a result of the Gaming Act 1968 (Variation of Monetary Limits) Order 2006[31].

MACHINES IN NON ALCOHOL-LICENSED PREMISES

The Gambling Act 2005 (Transitional Provisions) (No.2) Order 2006[32], which came into force on 1 August 2006, effectively banned the use of any such machines (on premises which were not subject to an alcohol licence) where the permit was issued by a licensing authority, with the exception of where the premises was a *bona fide* amusement arcade, under the following terms:

6.—*(1) This article applies to the grant or renewal of permits under section 34 of the 1968 Act by the authority mentioned in paragraph 1(b) or (d) of Schedule 9 to that Act(***c***) during the period beginning on the date on which*

---

29 Also known as fruit machines, jackpot machines.

30 On the use of tokens with gaming machines, see Capper v Baldwin [1965] 2 QB 53; [1965] 1 All ER 787.

31 SI 2006 2663.

32 SI 2006 1758.

this Order comes into force and ending on the date on which the repeal of that section and that Schedule by section 356(3)(g) and (4) of, and Schedule 17 to, the Gambling Act 2005 takes effect for all purposes. (2) Where the application is made on or after 1st August 2006, the authority may only grant or renew the permit if it relates to amusement machine premises.

The 2005 Act therefore removed approximately 6,000 fruit machines from premises such as take away food outlets, minicab and taxi offices, and other unlicensed premises where children could play them unsupervised[33]. From 31st July 2006 licensing authorities were unable to issue permits for gaming machines in these types of premises[34]. As the permits had a life span of three years, all of these machines were phased out by July 2009 as the final permits expired.

---

33 The continued use of machines on such premises was not seen as an attractive proposition as they were often used by children, whose access was not restricted. This was viewed as in contrast to the third licensing objective. See the DCMS fact sheet "Fruit Machines to be phased out of take away food shops and other non-arcade premises" July 2006.

34 In Scotland, this rule exacerbated a drafting error which meant that licensing boards could not issue permits to entertainment premises such as nightclubs. Only the local authority could issue the permits – and as a result of these transitional rules, the authority was then banned from doing so. This meant that pubs and bars, whose permits were issued by the licensing board, were safe, but existing permits for nightclubs could no longer be renewed.

NEW MACHINE CATEGORIES

The Gambling Act 2005 has dramatically changed how the use of gaming machines is regulated. Firstly, it has redefined the types of gaming machines that are general in use across the UK by creating four new categories of machine: A, B, C and D. The categories are as follows:

Category	**Maximum Stake**	**Maximum Prize**
A	Unlimited	Unlimited
B1	£2.00	£4000.00
B2	£100.00 (multiples of £10.00)	£500.00
B3A	£1.00	£500.00
B3	£1.00	£500.00
B4	£1.00	£250.00
C	50p	£35.00
D	10p	£5.00
D	30p (non monetary)	£8.00 (non monetary)

The only categories available to alcohol-licensed premises are C and D. The higher B3 and B4 categories are available to club premises (who may also provide C & D machines). The A machines are the preserve of casinos.

SKILL MACHINES

Before looking at the gaming machines allowed in alcohol-licensed premises, it is worth discussing "Skill Machines". Skill machines[35], including quiz games with a prize like the classic pub quiz machine, and machines such as arcade racing/space invader style machines, continue to be unregulated. However, the Gambling Commission are looking into

35 These are sometimes referred to as "Skill with Prizes" machines (SWPs). See The Gambling Commission's "Guidance to Licensing Authorities", 2nd Ed., June 2007: Page 94 paragraph 16.32.

machines which have a mixture of skill and an element of chance. They believe that certain machines which may appear or purport to be skill machines are actually not genuine "skill games" and are therefore machines fall within the definition of a "gaming machine" and are in turn regulated by the 2005 Act[36]. The Gambling Commission is currently working with the industry to try and produce a specification for true skill machines.

THE GAMING MACHINE CATEGORIES: A, B, C and D

The definitions of each of these categories are to be found in The Categories of Gaming Machine Regulations 2007[37]. We shall begin with the lowest form of machine, **Category D** machines. D machines are, in simple terms, machines which have either a "non-money" prize[38] machine where there maximum charge for use[39] is 30 pence and the maximum prize value[40] is £8; or a "money-prize" machine where the maximum charge for use is 10 pence and the maximum prize value is no more than £5. The definition of

---

36 On 13 July 2009 the Commission published an open letter to BACTA discussing their concerns on this point, and expressed the view that skill machines presented as games involving an element of chance would fall to be classed as gaming machines. They also raise concerns over the so-called "compensation mechanism" in some types of machines, which may introduce an element of chance.

37 SI 2007 2158.

38 "Prize" is defined in s.239 of the 2005 Act as "any money, article, right or service won, whether or not described as a prize, but ... (b) does not include an opportunity to play the machine again".

39 "Charge for use" in relation to any category of machine is defined in Article 2(1) of The Categories of Gaming Machines Regulations SI 2007 2158 as "the amount a person pays for using a gaming machine once". We would submit that the term "using a gaming machine" would constitute the participation in a/the "game". In Rosenbaum v Burgoyne [1965] AC 430 it was held that each pull of a gaming machine handle constituted a separate game. In modern times, this may be equivalent to the press of the "Start" or "Spin" button for those machines without an arm - in other words, each separate act of participation on the part of the player (Armstrong v DPP [1965] AC 1262) will constitute "using a gaming machine".

40 "Prize Value" in relation to any category of machine is defined in Article 2(1) of The Categories of Gaming Machines Regulations 2007 SI 2007 2158 as "the amount or value of any prize which can be won a result of use of a gaming machine once".

"money-prize" is found in Article 3(6) of the Regulations:

"(6) Subject to paragraph (7), in this regulation "money prize" means a prize—
(a) in the form of cash or a cheque (or partly in the form of cash and partly in the form of a cheque), or
(b) in the form of a document or object which—
(i) enables the person entitled to it to redeem its value, on the premises where the machine is made available for use, in the form of cash or a cheque (or partly in the form of cash and partly in the form of a cheque), and
(ii) may, but need not, also enable that person to use it to pay for goods or services available on the premises where the machine is made available for use, including facilities for gambling,
and "non-money prize" is any prize which is not a money prize.
(7) A document or object is not a money prize if it is something which ordinarily is capable of being used for a purpose other than one referred to in paragraph (6)(b).

Category D machines may be made available by casinos, betting premises, adult gaming centres, miner's welfare institutes, members' clubs, alcohol-licensed premises and family entertainment centres. The exact nature of Category D machines may require further elaboration. There are, we would suggest, four common types of Category D machines (and it should be noted that Category D includes such machines where the outcome is determined by mechanical means rather than computer automation):

- **Jackpot machines**: fruit machines or "one-armed bandit" style machines, albeit with lower stakes and prizes. These machines usually have some sort of theme and the action is based on nudges, holds, and other special features in an effort to spin three or four identical fruits or icons. This outcome may in itself provide a prize, but often now allows access to a further "game within a game" which may allow for higher prizes.

- **Cranes**: This a machine where a mechanical arm is manipulated by the user in order to try and "grab" some form of prize, usually a soft toy of some description. The crane is controlled by a joystick that the user positions over the prize of his choice, and then a button is pressed to lower the grabber. In order to win the prize, the prize must be successfully "grabbed" and lifted to a payout position in the corner of the machine.
- "**Multi-Slots**": the best example of this type of machine is the motorised horse racing or camel racing games where a coin is placed in one of five or so slots, each slot representing one of the runners in the game. The "runners" are models, affixed to an apparatus that guides them along a pre-set course. The outcome is predetermined randomly at the time of the start of the "race".
- **Pushers**: This type of machine usually consists of a moving deck, on which are pre-placed a number of coins (and sometimes other prizes) which seemingly defy gravity by perching on the ledge of the automated deck. The game player drops a coin in a slot of the top of the machine, hoping that it will fall behind those coins already on the deck, so that when the deck moves forward again it may "push" those coins on the edge over and into a tray for collection.

The Gambling Commission refers to the mechanised cranes, multi-slots and pushers as "Non Complex" Category D machines[41]. Operators should also note that these types of machines must display on their face a notice stating the following:

---

41 Gambling Commission publication "Machine Standards 'Non Complex' Category D", June 2007.

A **Category C** machine is simply described as a machine which has a maximum charge for use of no more than 50 pence; a maximum prize value of £35 and is not a Category D machine. This category caters for machines on alcohol-licensed premises, for which there is an "automatic entitlement" of up to two machines (See below). C machines are typically jackpot machines as described above (but with the higher stakes and prizes as noted previously).

Category B machines are slightly more complicated, as there are no less than five subdivisions in this category. The definitions are described in the regulations as follows:

- Category B4 is a machine with a maximum charge for use of £1 and a maximum prize value of £250 and is not a Category C or D machine. This is simply a higher class of traditional "Jackpot" machine.
- Category B3A is a machine with a maximum charge for use of £1 and a maximum prize value of £500, is not a Category B4, C or D machine, and enables a person to participate in a lottery but not any other form of gambling, and is made available for use by a members' club or a miner's welfare institute.
- Category B3 is a machine with a maximum charge for use of £1 and a maximum prize value of £500 but is not a B3A, B4, C or D machine. This is also a higher class of traditional "Jackpot" machine.
- Category B2 is a machine for which the maximum charge for use is no more than £100 and the maximum prize value is no more than £500, and is not a B3, B3A, B4, C or D machine. These machines are commonly known as "Fixed Odds Betting Terminals" (FOBTs) and are generally found in betting offices, for example in the form of

computerised roulette machines[42].

- Category B1 is a machine for which the maximum charge for use is no more than £2, the maximum prize value is £4000 and is not a B2, B3, B3A, B4, C or D machine. This is a high-class casino slot or jackpot machine.

The sub-categories of B machines relate, principally, to the type of premises on which they may be operated. It will be observed that B3A machines are lottery machines for use in member's clubs and miner's welfare institutes. Article 6 of the Regulations provides further guidance on the other subcategories of B machines:

- Adult Gaming Centres are allowed categories B3 and B4
- Casinos are allowed any category B machine except B3A
- Bingo premises are allowed B3 or B4 machines
- Betting premises are allowed B2, B3 or B4 machines
- Club Gaming and Club Machine Permits allow B3A or B4

Category A machines are simply defined as any machine which is not category B, C or D. These machines are only available to Regional Casinos.

It should be noted that there is an age restriction of 18 in respect of the playing of all of these categories of machines with the exception of category D, for which there is no age restriction. It should also be noted that where an alcohol-licensed premises has both C and D machines available (or B machines in clubs), they should be monitored in order to comply with the new Code of Practice[43] by preventing access to Category C machines to under 18s.

---

42 Machines which allow the gambler to place a stake on a real life event, such a roulette table in another part of a casino, do not fall to be classed as "gaming machines" and are dealt with under s.172 of the Act.

43 "Gaming Machine Permits Code of Practice" (June 2007). For a discussion on problems surrounding access, see the chapter on Family Entertainment Centres below.

ACCESS BY CHILDREN AND THE LICENSING ACT 2003

There is no requirement in the regulations to the Licensing Act 2003 to show areas to which children will be allowed to use or have access to in the layout plan required. This is unlike the position in Scotland where the premises licence "operating plan" requires the licence holder to specify which areas in the premises children and young persons will have access to. These areas must also be shown on the layout plan accompanying the premises licence north of the border.

In England and Wales, however, a different approach was taken and it may have been down to the fact that in many cases it would have been impractical with some pubs and clubs simply being too small to effectively ban children from these areas due to access and egress issues (a consideration ignored in Scotland!). However, where there is a mix of C, D (or B machines in clubs) then certainly we believe that, in order to adhere to the code, these should be located separately in order to maximise effective supervision.

Further, the Gambling Act 2005, has a perfectly good compliance mechanisms for situations in breach of a code or against the (gambling) licensing objectives[44]. The Gambling Commission's Gaming Machine Permits Code of Practice – Alcohol-licensed Premises Permits and Permissions, June 2007, has a section dedicated to access to gambling by children and young persons, which we would recommend to operators seeking to ensure compliance here.

---

44 For example, a licensing authority can remove the "automatic entitlement" to 2 machines under s.284 if an offence has been committed or the use of the entitlement is not consistent with the objectives.

GAMING MACHINES - CIRCUMSTANCES OF USE

There are further regulations regarding the use of machines under the new Act – namely The Gaming Machine (Circumstances of Use) Regulations 2007[45]. These regulations are mainly of a technical nature but are worth noting because they contain the rules regarding the display of information on machines, the nature of prizes and payment limits, machines with an "autoplay" feature, residues, and the delivery of winnings. The interested reader is advised to refer to the Regulations directly for more detail.

Also of relevance here is whether a single piece of apparatus which provides for more than player may be termed as "one machine". The answer is to be found in regulation 2 of the Gaming Machine (Single Apparatus) Regulations 2007[46] which states:

> *2. For the purposes of the Gambling Act 2005, where a single piece of apparatus is—*
> *(a) a gaming machine, and*
> *(b) made available for use to more than one person at a time,*
> *it is to be treated as the number of gaming machines equal to the number of people able to use it at that time.*

In other words, special machines which facilitate two or more persons playing at the same time are not to be counted as "one" machine, but as multiple machines based on the number of persons that may play.

45 SI 2007 2319.
46 SI 2007 2289.

GAMING MACHINES - "AVAILABLE FOR USE"

One of the terms which may require further elaboration in the context of gaming machines is "available for use". The starting point here is s.37(1)(c) of the Act, which makes it an offence to *use a premises for gambling* by making a gaming machine available for use. This is qualified by a number of exceptions under s.37(7) by referring to a series of further provisions, as follows:

- Where a family entertainment centre gaming machine permit is held (s.247)
- Where there is no prize available (s.248)
- Where the prize available does not exceed the amount staked (s.249)
- Where a club gaming permit is held (s.271)
- Where a club machine permit is held (s.273)
- Where an alcohol-licensed premises has activated the automatic entitlement (s.282)
- Where a Licensed Premises Gaming Machine Permit is held (s.283)
- Where, in respect of Category D machines only, the machines are provided at a travelling fair and the gambling is ancillary to the amusement available at the fair (s.287)

The position here is strengthened by s.242 which separately introduces a specific offence of *making a machine available for use*, unless one of the exceptions noted above applies. There is no further guidance on when exactly a machine can be considered to be "available for use" in the Act. Pertinently, the Gambling Commission has produced a guidance note to clarify the position, and they state: "*The Commission considers that a gaming machine is available for use if a person can play it*"[47].
The Commission note goes on to say that this does not preclude the

47 Gambling Commission Publication "Advice regarding when a machine is 'available for use'", December 2007.

physical positioning of a number of machines over those allowed by the permit or entitlement, so long as the relevant maximum is observed in terms of actual play and a robust management system is in place to ensure that these levels are not breached.

MACHINE REGULATIONS FOR PUBS AND CLUBS

With all of that in mind, we now turn to discuss the specific procedures for machines in pubs and clubs. The Licensed Premises Gaming Machine Permits (England and Wales) Regulations[48] and The Club Gaming and Club Machine Permits Regulations[49] both came into force on 1st August 2007.

The first thing to note is that not all alcohol-licensed premises in England and Wales can take up the entitlement or apply for a new permit. The machines may only be used by an on-premises alcohol licence which is defined in s.277(b) of the 2005 Act as meaning a premises licence under that Part which authorises the supply of alcohol for consumption on the licensed premises. Further, in accordance with s.278 the premises must contain a bar at which alcohol is served for consumption on the premises (without a requirement that alcohol is served only with food).

This need to have a bar in the premises will rule out some restaurants and certain bistro/cafe style premises from being able to obtain either an automatic entitlement or Licensed Premises Gaming Machine Permit (discussed below). Although "bar" is not defined in the 2005 Act as such, it is submitted that definition extends to genuine bars at which a customer can order and consumer alcohol, and that the test is not satisfied merely by the presence of a "serving" bar or other such facility which is only used by staff in order to provide table and waiter service.

48 SI 2007 1883.
49 SI 2007 1834.

THE NEW POSITION: TWO MACHINES OR LESS "NOTIFICATION"[50]

For the first time, there is now an automatic entitlement for any alcohol-licensed premises (noting the above exclusion) to have one or two machines, without need of any permit, licence, permission or renewal. All that is required is a one off payment of £50[51] and a letter to the appropriate licensing authority giving notice of the intent to take up the automatic entitlement under s.282 of the 2005 Act.

There was some confusion over whether there was an "application form" to complete to take advantage of the automatic entitlement. LACORS[52] issued a template form which the majority of the local authorities in England & Wales adopted.

The matter is clarified by the DCMS guidance document "Gambling Act 2005: Training Materials for Licensing Authorities" dated May 2007 which states that other than a letter and the fee "[T]*here is no other prescription regarding the form or content of the notification to be given*"[53]. In the result, if the relevant licensing authority has created a form then no doubt it will be prudent to make use of it, however it cannot be insisted on and the automatic entitlement can be requested with nothing other than a covering letter and a cheque for £50.

For those operators with an existing s.34 permit, that permit subsisted past

50 See also Arron, Nick (2007) "Legal Machinations", The Publican, 8th October 2007, Pg 52; http://tinyurl.com/2m4nzq.

51 The Gaming Machines in Alcohol-licensed Premises (Notification Fee)(England & Wales) Regulations, SI 2007 1832, Reg 3.

52 LACORS (Local Authorities Coordinators of Regulatory Services) is the local government central body responsible for overseeing local authority regulatory and related services.

53 At page 20, paragraph 6.

the big bang date of 1 September 2007 and retains the same expiry date[54]. The notice to take up the entitlement must be lodged with the board, along with the fee, prior to the existing date of expiry. As long as the notice is lodged in connection with a premises that holds a relevant alcohol licence, the automatic entitlement immediately applies and that premises has a lifetime permission[55] for up to 2 machines of either category C or D.

For new operators, you need merely send the notice and fee prior to making the machines available. In the absence of an application form for this procedure[56] it may be prudent to indicate on the notification letter how many machines you are making available and of what category. This also applies to persons taking over a currently licensed premises with automatic entitlement – a fresh notification and fee of £50 is required every time the premises changes hands (presuming that the premises licence holder is to be changed by way of application for transfer under the Licensing Act 2003).

Although the automatic entitlement cannot be refused, the Act has not completely removed power from the hands of the licensing authority over the provision of 2 or less machines. Under s.284 of the Act a licensing authority may make an order to disapply the automatic entitlement on one of the following four grounds:

- The entitlement is not reasonably consistent with the licensing objectives.
- That gaming is taking place in breach of a condition.
- That the premises is mainly used for gaming.
- Where an offence has been committed on the premises.

---

54 If a permit has been issued with no expiry date, or no expiry date is showing on the permit, it is deemed to have an expiry date of 31st August 2010.

55 Unless the premises changes hands, in which case a fresh entitlement request is required.

56 It does seem strange that no statutory form was created for this procedure, as everything else in the world of licensing and gambling has an application form to complete!

If such an order is made, the operator must be given 21 days' notice, the operator may request a hearing, and the decision may be appealed.

It has been proposed by some that a licensing authority may use the disapplying power under s.284 to "refuse" a notification for automatic entitlement. In our view, this approach is wrong. This power can only be used where the automatic entitlement is already in force. In order for the automatic entitlement to be "disapplied", it must first have been activated; and then should only be disapplied on the basis that one of the four grounds above can be borne out.

For the notification of intent to offer 1 or 2 gaming machines the licensing authority may issue an acknowledgement which should be retained by the applicant on the premises for inspection. If there is no attached form asking for acknowledgement from the licensing authority and no reference to acknowledgement in any attached guidance it would be sensible to enclose with the application form a request for acknowledgment. This should then be retained by the applicant on the premises for inspection.

AUTOMATIC ENTITLEMENT – FEES

As mentioned, there is a one off fee of £50 to be paid to the relevant council when the request is first made. There is no further fee whatsoever, unless the premises changes hands and a new operator comes in, in which event a fresh request with a further £50 would be required.

THE NEW POSITION: THREE MACHINES OR MORE

The matter is slightly more complicated if an operator has, or wishes to have, three or more machines. If that is the case, a Licensed Premises Gaming Machine Permit is required. This is processed by way of application to the relevant licensing authority– for existing holders of s.34 permits, any time prior to the expiry of their current permit, and for new applicants at any time but clearly in advance of making the machines available for use. Existing operators will have continuation rights, meaning they can continue to use the same number and type of machines they have currently until the new application has been resolved.

LICENSED PREMISES GAMING MACHINE PERMITS – APPLICATION PROCEDURE

The new permit has some new features, previously unavailable under the old s.34 permit. Firstly, the permit will last indefinitely, removing the previous lifespan of 3 years. Another advance here is the ability to "transfer" a gaming permit under the new Act, a facility unavailable under the previous regime. The permit may be varied by way of application (attracting a fee of £100) with respect to either number of machines, category of machine, or both.

The Gambling Act 2005 makes no provision for a requirement to supplement the LPGMP with as plan; and the LACORS policy forum also expressed the view that a plan would not be required with an application. However, for mixed use premises (e.g. a bowling alley) it may be the case that a plan showing the intended licensed area and proposed location of machines may be appropriate. All applicants are urged to check the application form carefully in order to ascertain if a plan is or is not required.

Unlike the automatic entitlement procedure where there is no requirement to use the form specified by the licensing authority, for new applications, variations, transfer and conversion applications the 2005 Act allows licensing authorities to specify the form and manner of applications and any information/documentation to be provided. If these requirements are not met then the application has not been correctly made.

LICENSED PREMISES GAMING MACHINE PERMITS – FEES

A new grant of a LPGMP is £150[57], although there is a reduced fee of £100 for current s.34 permit holders upon conversion[58]. As the permit lasts indefinitely there is no renewal fee, however there is annual fee of £50, which must be paid within 30 days of the initial grant or conversion issue date[59], and then every year within 30 days of the "anniversary" date of the permit[60]. A transfer application costs £25[61] and a variation application £100[62]. A duplicate copy of the permit costs £15[63].

Finally, each licensing authority must maintain a register of permits issued.

CLUB PERMITS

There are two types of Club Permits under the new regime: **Club Machine Permits**; and **Club Gaming Permits**. The Act lays down statutory definitions for three types of such premises which are important as not all can apply for the different types of permits[64]. The three types

---

57 Licensed Premises Gaming Machines Permits (England and Wales) Regulations 2007, SI 2007 1833, reg 3(a)(ii).
58 Ibid, reg 3(a)(i).
59 Ibid, reg 7(1).
60 Ibid, reg 7.
61 Ibid, reg 3(c).
62 Ibid, reg 3(b).
63 Ibid, reg 9.
64 It is hoped that these specific definitions will avoid the infamously un-navigable case law that resulted from Part III Registrations under the 1968 Act: Tehrani v Rostron [1972] 1 QB 182; [1971] 3 All ER 790 CA, Miriam Walters v The Chief Constable of Nottingham, 14 October 1975, and Chief Constable of Strathclyde Police v Pollokshaws Road Snooker Centre [1977] SLT (Sh.Ct) 72 all being examples.

are: "**members' clubs**"; "**commercial clubs**" and "**miner's welfare institutes**". The definition of each is as follows:

Members' Club

Under s.266, a members' club is a club which:

- Is established and conducted wholly or mainly for purposes other than the provision of facilities for gaming (other than Bridge or Whist)
- Is established and conducted for the benefit of its members (and which is not otherwise established or conducted as a commercial enterprise)
- Is not established with the purpose of functioning only for a limited period of time
- Has at least 25 members

Members ' clubs may apply to their local licensing authority for both club gaming permits and club machine permits.

The Gambling Commission suggests that premises such as working men's clubs, Royal British Legion clubs and clubs with political affiliations will fall within this definition[65].

Commercial Club

Defined under s.267, a commercial club is a club which:

- Is established and conducted wholly or mainly for purposes other than the provision of facilities for gaming (other than Bridge or Whist)
- Is not established with the purpose of functioning only for a limited period of time
- Has at least 25 members

---

65 Gambling Commission Publication "Advice on Gaming in Clubs and Alcohol-licensed Premises", September 2008, page 2 paragraph 2.3.

Commercial clubs may only apply for club machine permits and are prevented from applying for club gaming permits.

Examples of a "commercial club" include snooker clubs, clubs established as private companies and any club established for personal profit – whether that profit is made or not!

Miners' Welfare Institute

This final class of "club" falls to be defined under s.268 of the 2005 Act and is an association which:

- Is established and conducted for social and recreational purposes; and is EITHER
- Managed by a group of individuals of whom at least two thirds are miners' representatives[66]; OR
- Operates on premises the use of which is regulated in accordance with a charitable trust[67]

Miners' welfare institutes may apply for both a club gaming permit and a club machine permit.

Having considered the definitions of these, the relevance is that only a members' club or miner's welfare institute may apply for a club gaming permit, whereas all three may apply for a club machine permit.

CLUB MACHINE PERMITS

The Gambling Act 2005 has replaced the old style permits traditionally associated with clubs known in licensing circles simply as "Part III"

66 See s.268(3) for the definition of "miners' representative".
67 Under s.268(4)(b) the trust has to have received money from certain organisations which are listed.

machines[68]. These machines are basically jackpot machines but with a higher stake and maximum payout, which can range from upwards of 50p and £250 respectively. The permission for use of these machines, which were dealt with by way of registration by the jurisdictional Betting, Gaming and Licensing Committee, has been moved to the relevant licensing authority under a new permit called a Club Machine Permit. A Club Machine Permit can allow up to a maximum of three Category B4, C or D machines (see the category guidance above) and is therefore broadly equitable to the Part III registration.

Club Machine Permits may be used by a members' club, a commercial club or a miner's welfare institute, in "the course of activities of the club or institute"[69]

A licensing authority has no discretion to add additional conditions to a club machine permit, but three conditions will automatically apply through s.273 which lays down some restrictions on the use of the machines:

- Each permit is subject to a condition that any person to whom a machine is made available for use is either a member of the club or institute (and has been for at least 48 hours), or his *bona fide* guest[70]
- No child or young person may use a B or C machine on the premises and that the holder complies with the Code of Practice in relation to the location of the machines (see below).
- That the club complies with any codes of practice issued by the Gambling Commission about the location and operation of its gaming machines.

The Permit will not authorize any other facility for gaming.

---

68 As they were regulated under Part III of the Gaming Act 1968.

69 S.273(2(b).

70 s.273(5) gives further guidance on what may constitute a genuine guest. There must be a previous acquaintance between the member and guest, and the invitation to enter the establishment cannot be for the purpose of enabling the person to "take advantage of the facilities for gaming".

CLUB GAMING PERMITS

The registration under Part II of the old 1968 Act has now become facilitated by way of a new creation called a Club Gaming Permit, which is a higher class of permit that can only be held by member's clubs or miner's welfare institutes (not commercial clubs)[71]. This type of Permit allows the provision of no more than 3 B3A machines but also equal chance gaming *without prescribed limitations on prizes or stakes*[72].

Such a permit would appear to be of obvious use to premises such as a poker club whose operators would seek to avoid the constraints of the Equal Chance Gaming regulations discussed below, but the permit cannot be used if the club is devoted "wholly or mainly" to providing that form of gaming (see the paragraph on "Private Poker Clubs" below), due to the restriction in the definition of "member's club" under s. 266(1)(a) of the 2005 Act.

However, under the Code of Practice for Equal Chance Gaming, a premises which holds a Club Gaming permit may also offer two types of banker's games: pontoon[73], and *chemin de fer*[74]. This type of permit clearly provides for the operation of poker nights with unlimited stakes and prizes in clubs so long as they are *bona fide* member's clubs, stay within the conditions of the permit and Code of Practice, and are not too regular.

---

71 The Gambling Commission has produced a series of questions which licensing authorities may use to assist themselves in determining whether a club is a bona fide members' club or not: see the publication "Advice to Licensing Authorities on Club Gaming Permits and Club Machine Permits: Gambling Act 2005" Pg 4 Para 4.1(a)

72 S.279.

73 A variant of the wider known games "blackjack" or "21".

74 *Chemin de fer* is a variant of baccarat, which in very simple terms is a card game with a banker and a number of players in which two cards are dealt, the aim being to achieve an eight or nine and placing stakes accordingly.

s.271(4) of the Act lays down some restrictions of the provision of gaming using this type of permit:

- No participation fee can be charged other than in accordance with regulations
- No amount can be deducted or levied from sums staked or won other that in accordance with regulations
- The public must be excluded from the area the gaming is taking place[75]
- Children and young persons must be excluded from the area the gaming is taking place

The participation fee is laid down in the Gambling Act 2005 (Club Gaming Permits) (Authorised Gaming) Regulations 2007[76] and is set as a maximum of £3 per day. There are no regulations to date regarding amounts which may be deducted or levied, so that in fact no amount may be deducted or levied[77].

CLUB PERMITS - APPLICATION PROCEDURE

Applications for both the Club Gaming Permit and the Club Machine Permit are made to the relevant licensing authority and within seven days a copy must be sent to the Chief Constable and the Gambling Commission[78]. Club Permits may be varied upon application, and unlike the

75 S.271(6) gives guidance on who may or may not be "the public" – participation is restricted to members and bona fide guests of members. As with the restrictions discussed above for Club Machine Permits, members must be as such for at least 48 hours before they can make use of gaming facilities.

76 SI 2007 1945.

77 See the Gambling Commission publication "Advice on gaming in clubs and alcohol-licensed premises: Gambling Act 2005", December 2007 Pg 3, Para 3.1(a).

78 For guidance on appeals, see Gambling Commission publication "Advice to Licensing Authorities on Club Gaming Permits and Club Machine Permits : Gambling Act 2005", December 2007 Pg 6, Para 7.

Licensed Premises Gaming Machine Permit, which is of infinite duration, have a lifespan of ten years – at which point they require to be renewed.

A renewal must be lodged no sooner than three months but no later than six weeks prior to the date of expiry, and article 20 of the regulations makes provision for a permit to remain "live" past any expiry if a renewal application has been lodged and is pending[79]. The licensing authority must keep a register of both types of Club Permit.

There is no transfer facility for club permits so if a club premises ever changed hands and a new operator became required then a brand new grant of club permit would be required.

For existing operators of permissions under Part II or III of the Gaming Act 1968, these were automatically converted to a Club Gaming Permit or Club Machine Permit on 1 September 2007 and the expiry date remains the same. The matter of when a "conversion" application from the existing Part II or III registration to a new Club Gaming or Club Machine Permit was subject to some change as a result of various transitional provisions and the matter was not altogether clear. As mentioned in connection with Licensed Premises Gaming Machine Permits, many local authorities were advising in December 2007 that the "conversion" application had to be lodged two months before the expiry date of the existing Part II or III registration.

This position was no doubt based on the terms of the Club Gaming and Club Machine Permits Regulations 2007[80], which say that existing operators must apply for their conversions with reference to a "relevant date" under paragraph 88(3) to (5) of Schedule 4 to the Gambling Act

79 Or where an application for renewal has been refused, but has been appealed and that appeal has not yet been determined.
80 SI 2007 1834.

2005 (Commencement No. 6 and Transitional Provisions) Order 2006[81], which is as follows (our emphasis):

> ***88.** —(1) Subject to the following provisions of this Part, where—*
> *(a) a members' club, commercial club or miners' welfare institute applies to the relevant licensing authority for the grant of a club machine permit in respect of the same or substantially the same premises as those to which the registration under Part 3 of the 1968 Act relates;*
>
> *(b) the application complies with sub-paragraphs (b) and (e) of paragraph 2 and (where applicable) paragraph 3 of Schedule 12 to the 2005 Act; and*
>
> *(c) the application is made* **not less than two months** *before the relevant date*
> *the relevant licensing authority* **must** *grant that application.*

And then goes on to say:

> *(3) Subject to sub-paragraphs (4) and (5), in sub-paragraph (1)(c) "the relevant date"* **means the date on which the club or institute's registration, as it had immediately before 1st September 2007, was due to expire** *in accordance with paragraph 22 of Schedule 7 to the 1968 Act…*

In short, "conversion" applications had to be lodged two months in advance of the existing Part II or III expiry date. But there some circumstances were the expiry date of the existing permit occurred prior to these regulations coming into force, and as such there seemed to be no route for an operator to submit an appropriate application.

---

81 SI 2006 3272.

In those circumstances a further transitional arrangement was included in the above Order to provide some comfort. Paragraph 93(3) and (4) of the 2006 Order state that if the regulations were late in coming in to force, then the last lodgement date for the conversion application would be either two months before the existing expiry, or **one month from the date of the regulations coming in to force**, which ever was the nearer.

This "safety valve" mechanism was probably missed by most operators and local authority staff, and in any event the whole matter was further reconfigured by a later amending instrument, The Gambling Act 2005 (Commencement and Transitional Provisions) (Amendment) Order 2007[82] which in the result amended the 2006 Order by deleting the words "***not less than two months***" from Paragraph 88(1)(c) as well as all other references to the two month notice.

The effect of this tortuous process is that the conversion application to change an existing Part II or Part III registration to a Club Gaming or Club Machine Permit can be lodged **at any time** prior to the existing expiry date of that registration.

Finally, note that there is a "variation procedure" under article 15 of the Club Regulations whereby if any information on the permits ceases to be accurate, a variation application must be lodged along with the permit itself. The licensing authority has the power to refuse the variation and cancel the permit if it would have refused it as a new application.

FEES FOR CLUB PERMITS

The Gambling Act 2005 (Club Gaming and Club Machine Permits) Regulations 2007 lay down a fee of £200 for the grant or renewal of a

82 SI 2007 1157.

Club Machine/Gaming Permit, however a reduced fee of £100 if available if the applicant was an existing Part II or Part III operator. There is also an annual fee of £50, which must be paid within 30 days of the initial grant or conversion issue date, and then every year within 30 days of the "anniversary" date of the permit. The cost of a variation of a Club Machine/Gaming Permit is £100; and a renewal is £200.

GAMING MACHINE PERMITS CODE OF PRACTICE

This code was first issued in June 2007 (coming into force on 1 September 2007) and relates to: **machines under automatic entitlement**; **licensed premises gaming machine permits**; **club machine permits**; and **club gaming permits**. There are two provisions of this code of practice which are a condition of the permit, which are as follows:

- All gaming machines situated on the premises must be located in a place within the premises so that their use can be supervised, either by staff whose duties include such supervision (including bar or floor staff) or by other means. Permit holders must have arrangements in place to ensure effective supervision.
- All gaming machines situated on the premises shall be located in a place that requires a customer who wishes to use any ATM made available on the premises to cease gambling at the gaming machine in order to do so. "ATM" means a machine located on the premises, which enables a person using it to obtain cash by using a credit or debit card.

Failure to comply with these provisions could result in revocation of the permit. Further, the Code lists a series of secondary provisions, which although are not conditions, are considered "best practice". There are two main thrusts to these, which are: to prevent under age gambling; and to help and assist "self exclusion".

The code expects machine operators to monitor any Category C or higher machines available so that they are not used by children or young persons; by having procedures to check a person's age, and even a warning system if a particular child or young person is caught using a machine more than one occasion.

In relation to "self exclusion", the code expects operators to monitor those seeking to use the machines in order to prevent a person who appears to be a problem gambler from participating – in other words, to have the person stop playing the machine. It is recommended that operators keep a logbook to show if they have refused service, and note if a "self exclusion" agreement has been agreed to by the operator and a vulnerable gambler as to whether access is prevented, or restricted to a certain period.

In February and March 2008, the concept of "self exclusion" was very much in the eyes of the media, as self-confessed habitual gambler Graham Calvert pursued an action against William Hill after they failed to honour a self exclusion policy which had been set up to stop the bookmakers taking any further bets from him. He was allowed to continue to gamble, and lost some £2.1million. William Hill did not deny that they had continued to allow him to gamble, but instead relied on the defence that they owed him no special duty of care because he was a problem gambler. In the result, Mr Justice Briggs agreed with the bookmaker and threw the claim out, reasoning that Mr Calvert would have simply lost the money gambling elsewhere[83].

However, he did go on to say in his judgement: "*The self-exclusion procedure forms a main plank in the social responsibility structure which stands as the quid per quo for the modern policy of the encouragement of gambling as an industry and as a leisure activity. The question whether the limited effectiveness*

83 Calvert v William Hill Ltd [2008] EWHC 454 (Ch).

of self-exclusion as a remedy for problem gambling undermines the integrity of that public policy bargain is something for the Gambling Commission and Parliament rather than the courts to decide"[84].

The effectiveness of the self exclusion policy, when not observed, would therefore seem to have a somewhat limited reach when there is no sanction against a provider of gambling services who fails to observe the agreement.

84 Ibid., at para 220.

CHAPTER FIVE
EQUAL CHANCE GAMING (INCLUDING POKER)

The term "Equal Chance Gaming" is defined in s.8 of the Act in the following terms:

(1) For the purposes of this Act gaming is equal chance gaming if—
(a) it does not involve playing or staking against a bank, and
(b) the chances are equally favourable to all participants
(2) For the purposes of subsection (1) it is immaterial—
(a) how a bank is described, and
(b) whether or not a bank is controlled or administered by a player

This can, of course, apply to a number of games without a banker; for example bingo, bridge, dominoes or cribbage - but has now come to be most associated with poker.

POKER GAMES UNDER THE GAMING ACT 1968

Texas Hold 'Em No Limits poker has been a modern business success story. The popularity of this specific form of poker has reached incredible heights and the game can be seen on television shows as well as in casinos, on-line, and in private domestic settings between friends.

Many licensed trade operators, sensing a potential market to boost their trade following the smoking bans on 26 March 2006 in Scotland, 2 April

2007 in Wales, and finally 1 July 2007 in England, took advantage and began promoting "poker nights" in their bars and clubs. The position prior to 1 September 2007 was contained in the Gaming Act 1968, and specifically in Section 6, which allowed a licence holder to apply to the relevant licensing authority for an order under Section 6(3) permitting the playing of games for small stakes. There were a number of restrictions:

- Banker's games were prohibited
- the game must provide all players with an equal chance
- no charge for participation could be made
- there could be no levy on winnings, and
- the provision of gaming could not constitute an inducement to resort to the premises

The aim of a poker night was to boost trade, but the inability to advertise or promote the game as an attraction would frustrate its purpose.

What about games with no cash prizes? Permission for poker playing would only be required by the 1968 Act if it was being played for money or money's worth - money's worth is given the common law definition and would include emoluments, vouchers, goods or other items which have a value. There are poker leagues in operation where individuals play for points rather than prizes so that there is no "gaming" taking place. But poker will not normally be a big 'draw' unless there is a prospect of financial benefit. Section 40 of the 1968 Act allowed clubs, including proprietary clubs, to impose small charges for participation in non-banker games of equal chance. The original purpose of this provision was to cater for specialist bridge and whist clubs, but it became a popular vehicle for bingo and was utilised for poker games.

PRIVATE POKER CLUBS

Private poker clubs also came into existence, as the poker boom did not subside. Owners of some such establishments claimed that they were not breaking the law because poker is a game of skill, rather than chance. However, many police forces were not of the same opinion and pursued convictions for gaming offences.

On 16 January 2007 Derek Kelly, chairman of the "Gutshot Club"[85] in London was found guilty of poker offences under the 1968 Act after he organised and ran two unlicensed poker games from which he profited through entry fees and a table rake. Mr Kelly tried to argue that poker was a game of skill rather than chance[86], and therefore out-with the ambit of the 1968 Act, but failed and was convicted. The judge said: "*This could have caused enormous problems for the gaming industry and given the green light for unregulated poker. I consider the prosecution were right to take this matter seriously*".

The Gambling Commission was "*pleased to see the case concluded*". A spokesperson said:

"*The Gaming Act 1968 has always been clear ... commercial gaming needs to be undertaken in a properly regulated environment to ensure that members of the public are protected from cheating and exploitation. The Gutshot has operated as a poker club with few membership or entry controls. Its facilities are very limited and its player protections would not meet expected standards… Poker is a very popular game, but those involved as players or*

---

85 Gutshot" is a poker term for the occasion when you receive a middle card to complete a straight.

86 See http://news.bbc.co.uk/1/hi/england/london/6267603.stm, and Lippiet, Tom (2007) "Is poker a game of skill or chance?", Sport & Technology, February 2007, http://www.sportandtechnology.com/features/0460.html.

organisers in games where significant sums of money may be involved need to be aware that without proper supervision it can rapidly escalate into a high risk, volatile activity, as well as create opportunities for criminal exploitation and cheating".

Further, The Gambling Commission's position, which persisted until the summer of 2007, was that "*no effective limitation of stakes is practicable*" and that the playing of poker was liable to lead to "*exploitation and disorder*".

Despite this scaremongering, the game of poker has held its cards well (so to speak) and the hybrid status of chance and skill is now enshrined in s.6 of the Gambling Act which defines "gaming" as a "game of chance". This in turn is defined as a game that involves "*both an element of chance and an element of skill; or a game that involves an element of chance which can be eliminated by superlative skill*", and further, in the DCMS fact sheet on poker (issued in August 2007) it is described as: "*a card game which, like bridge, involves elements of both chance and skill*"[87].

The position of "poker clubs" seeking to provide unlimited stakes and prizes has, however, been limited as the permit which would allow this - a Club Gaming Permit - may not be applied for where gaming is the main activity[88] of the club – and note further that commercial clubs[89] are prohibited from applying for these types of permit under s.271(2)(a) of the 2005 Act. The Gambling Commission has said: "*licensing authorities must satisfy themselves that the club is not wholly or mainly devoted to*

87 Indeed, an appeal by Mr Kelly was over-ruled on 14th February 2008, the appeal court finding that the jury had been properly directed that poker was a game of chance for the purposes of s..52(1) of the Gaming Act 1968, which states that "'*game of chance'…includes a game of chance and skill combined and a pretended game of skill and chance combined*".

88 For further information on this point, refer to the Gambling Commission publication "Advice on gaming in clubs and alcohol-licensed premises: Gambling Act 2005", December 2007 Pg, Para 2.5

89 Defined in s.267 of the 2005 Act.

poker…[T]hose clubs who hold club gaming permits and conduct themselves in such a way that gaming (poker) is the main activity are in breach of the Act and may render themselves liable to prosecution"[90]. For more on this, see the section relating to Club Gaming Permits, in Chapter 4 above.

DCMS CONSULTATION ON POKER

The Government, in the run up to the introduction of the 2005 Act, had ignored all the sabre-rattling and DCMS launched a consultation regarding regulations allowing poker in alcohol-licensed premises. Referring to "*significant recent growth*" in the game's popularity, the DCMS consultation document saw "*a need to address the particular risks associated with such gaming*".

The DCMS proposals were not greeted with universal enthusiasm. Opponents said that the Government was creating a recipe for a dangerous cocktail of alcohol and gaming: the more people drink heavily, the more their judgment is impaired. Regardless, and in spite of the furore, the consultation ended in the issue of two regulations: The Gambling Act 2005 (Exempt Gaming in Alcohol-licensed Premises) Regulations 2007[91] and The Gambling Act 2005 (Exempt Gaming in Clubs) Regulations 2007[92].

90 Gambling Commission publication "Advice to Licensing Authorities on Club Gaming Permits and Club Machine Permits: Gambling Act 2005" December 2007, Pg 2 para 1.4.

91 SI 2007 1940. There was a reference to a mysterious "paragraph 4" in this instrument. References to this elusive paragraph, which did not in fact exist, were later deleted by way of a further amending instrument, The Gambling Act (Exempt Gaming in Alcohol-Licensed Premises) (Amendment) SI 2007 2240.

92 SI 2007 1944.

THE "EXEMPT GAMING" REGULATIONS

The alcohol-licensed premises regulations are concise and simply facilitate the legalisation of poker by using the exemption power under s.279 of the 2005 Act, which authorises such premises to provide facilities for equal chance gaming without any further licence or permission requirement. The regulations limit the maximum stake on any form of equal chance gaming (including poker) to £5 (except those hardy classics, cribbage and dominoes); and further that the aggregate amount that may be staked on games of poker in one day may not exceed £100. This means that there a maximum of 20 players per game of poker must be observed, presuming each person has the chance to stake up to the maximum £5. The maximum prize allowed is also £100.

The Club Regulations, whilst allowing for greater stakes and prizes, are more prescriptive[93]. In club premises, the maximum that can be staked by a person on any game of poker must not exceed £10; the aggregate amount staked in one day must not exceed £250, and the aggregate amount that may be staked in seven days must not exceed £1000. Further, the maximum prize that may be won is £250. Remember that these prescribed limits do not apply if the premises holds a Club Gaming Permit.

The amount a club may charge for participation also depends on whether they also hold a Club Gaming Permit. If no permit is in place, a club may charge £18 in respect of bridge or whist so long as no other forms of gaming are also available; or in any other case £1. If a permit is in place, then may charge £20 and £3 accordingly[94].

---

93 These rules apply to member's clubs, commercial clubs and miner's welfare institutes. See s.266(1)(a) and s.267(1)(b) for further guidance on what constitutes a members club and commercial club respectively.

94 There are subdivisions here between commercial clubs and other forms of club in relation to Value Added Tax. See Reg 4 & 5 for more detail.

The outcome of all of this is of course the legalisation of poker, with monetary limits in most circumstances, in alcohol-licensed premises and certain clubs from 1 September 2007 and operators such as Rileys Snooker Clubs and many others have been quick to capitalise on this, setting up a number of leagues across the UK[95].

THE POKER RULES IN PRACTICE

It is important to remember that the stakes limit of £5 for pubs and £10 for clubs is per person **per game**. It is worth briefly discussing what is meant by "game" in this context. A "game" is not merely *a hand* of poker, but can constitute *several hands* over the course of play. In such circumstances where one player has won several games in one evening, leading to a final in a knockout tournament perhaps, then he could be capable of winning several hundreds of pounds - so long as the individual games did not breach the £100 maximum prize and so long as he personally has not staked more than £100 in one day.

The salient point here is that although the £100 maximum for stakes is per day, the £100 maximum for prizes is not limited by **day** but by **game**, as laid down in the Regulations:

> Requirements in relation to poker prize
> 3.—(1) For the purposes of section 279(2)(b) of the Act, the maximum amount or value of a prize that may be won in any game of poker is £100.

So, where an individual has played four games to reach a final, he could have already won up to £400 (having played four separate games and

95 There was some outcry from the mainstream licensed trade about the policy reasons behind allowing clubs to have higher stakes and prizes. See for example: Wimore, James (2007) "Government accused of favouring clubs in new gaming rules", The Publican, 26th April 2007 http://www.thepublican.com/story.asp?storyCode=55164

winning £100 in each); but again the maximum he could win in the final is another £100[96]. It is quite conceivable for a skilled poker player to have come to the table with £5 and slowly won his way up to £400 in prizes in the course of one day having staked nothing further of his own cash. The same principle, of course, applies to clubs but with the higher values for stakes and prizes noted above.

Operators of poker nights should have regard to the Gambling Commission guidance documentation on the practicalities of running such nights, including the special guidance note "Poker in Pubs" published in July 2009[97], which provides useful information on how tournament play may be facilitated.

EQUAL CHANCE GAMING ON ALCOHOL-LICENSED PREMISES CODE OF PRACTICE

The Gambling Commission issued a Code of Practice in July 2007 which introduces further rules to be observed here. The observance of the code is remitted to the "Designated Premises Supervisor" (a role created under the Licensing Act 2003 which means the person nominated as such in connection with the alcohol premises licence). This person now enjoys the added sobriquet of "gaming supervisor", and their duties will include the following:

- Ensuring compliance with maximum stakes as laid down by the regulations
- Ensuring that gaming is supervised
- Ensuring that no under age gaming takes place

96 For more details on the technicalities of how prizes should be distributed in tournament play, see the Gambling Commission publication "Advice on Gaming in Clubs and Alcohol-licensed Premises", December 2007, Page 4 Paras 5.1 through 5.5.

97 Ref ADV09/06.

- All payments must be made in cash and no credit facilities can be offered
- Gaming equipment should be locked up when not in use
- The gaming rules should be displayed
- The gaming supervisor should promote a pleasant atmosphere and deny participation to cheaters and colluders

There are specific provisions for poker:

- It is recommended that "cash" games should not be permitted, in other words, that no money should be on the table
- The premises should supply its own poker chips for use instead of money
- The maximum stakes and prizes are per game, not per hand
- A record must be kept of the number of games; the number of players; and amounts staked; to ensure the stake and prize limits are not exceeded
- The gaming supervisor must take reasonable steps to ensure the limits are not breached

If you are the operator of an alcohol-licensed premises and you hire an external organisation to provide and run your poker nights, remember that the onus is still on you to ensure that these rules and conditions are met.

CHAPTER SIX
NON-COMMERCIAL & EXEMPT GAMING IN ALCOHOL-LICENSED PREMISES

For years "Casino Nights", "Vegas Night", or other such gambling themed nights – even where for charitable purposes – have been a cause for concern when held on alcohol-licensed premises for some parties. This did not stop many schemes coming forward with play "for fun" or on the basis of a competition with the "best gambler of the night" winning a prize which varied in its value.

Another popular example which occurs frequently in alcohol-licensed premises is "Race Night" where pre-recorded footage of horse or dog racing is shown in a bar and patrons gamble. This has regularly been used as the basis for a charity event.

The uncertainty over the legal position here led to a considerable gray area and confusion in what was lawful, both by operators and enforcement officers alike.

No doubt to the dismay of certain groups, the 2005 Act has changed all of that and clarified the position. Section 279 specifically allows gaming on alcohol-licensed premises, with limits on stakes, under the auspices of the equal chance gaming regulations (which also provide for poker as discussed above). There is further provision for gambling where the aim is to raise money for a "specified purpose" (in other words, charity nights). In these circumstances the Act has removed the general offence of providing gambling without holding an operating licence under s.33, where that gambling is on alcohol-licensed premises and complies with statutory provisions.

EXEMPT GAMING

The exempt gaming rules are the rules which allow equal chance gaming as has been previously discussed in relation to poker. They are treated separately here by virtue of the fact that most operators and authorities view the themed "gambling" night as separate from a poker night.

- The gaming must comply with the regulations noted below
- There can be no levy
- There can be no entry or participation fee
- The gaming cannot be linked to gaming on other premises
- The gaming is restricted to over 18s only

Operators are still bound by the ethos that responsible gaming is paramount. The local authority may strip alcohol-licensed premises of their ability to provide gaming under s.279 if it believes gaming has taken place in breach of one of the above conditions, or if it thinks it best to remove the exemption in the interest of the licensing objectives, using provisions in s.284 (the same power which can be used to disapply the automatic entitlement to 2 gaming machines). If the local authority is of a mind to make an order disapplying s.279, it must give the operator 21 days' notice and the decision may be appealed. The premises licence under the Licensing Act 2003 would also be at risk if breaches of the licensing objectives can be seen as a result of irresponsible/illegal gaming taking place on the premises.

The types of gaming allowed are effectively any which do not involve a banker[98] and the gaming must be ancillary to the purpose of the premises – just as with poker, the premises could not be used as an "exempt gaming" club where the gaming is wholly or mainly the purpose for the premises.

EXEMPT GAMING FOR A SPECIFIED PURPOSE

The exemption for "non-commercial gaming", as it is known in this context, can only apply to prize gaming or equal chance gaming and is, it is submitted, is the avenue for special "charity nights" in alcohol-licensed premises and clubs. Under s.300, the following conditions must be observed:

- Players must be informed that the purpose of the gaming is to raise money for a specified purpose other than that of private gain
- The arrangements for the gaming are such that the profits will be applied for a purpose other than that of private gain
- The event cannot take place on a premises for which a premises licence or temporary use notice[99] has effect[100]
- The gaming cannot be remote

These rules apply to non-commercial equal chance gaming and non-commercial prize gaming. For non-commercial *equal chance* gaming, there is an additional rule to be observed:

- The arrangements for the gaming ensure compliance with regulations regarding the amount of stakes, fees and other paid amounts

---

98 Examples of typical banker's games are blackjack, or roulette.
99 See chapter 12 on temporary use notices.
100 There are further qualifications for tracks, see s.299(4).

If an operator is found to be using profits for something other then the specified purpose, he is committing an offence under s.301. The maximum amount which can be staked and the amount considered to be "costs reasonably incurred" are found in the Gambling Act 2005 (Non-Commercial Equal Chance Gaming) Regulations 2007[101]. This instrument adds the following rules to be observed:

- Only one payment per person may be requested to participate in a non-commercial gaming event
- That payment may not exceed £8
- The aggregate amount for all prizes available for winning in that event may not exceed £600
- If there is a series of linked events, which occur on more than one day, no more than £8 can be requested in stakes per day and the prizes available at the final event may not exceed £900

These regulations came into force on 1 September 2007 and we have been unable to find any prosecution for breach of the Regulations at the time of writing.

101 SI 2007 2041.

CHAPTER SEVEN
LOTTERIES IN ALCOHOL-LICENSED PREMISES

The law relating to lotteries in the United Kingdom is very strict and it is an offence to promote a lottery unless it is promoted by the holder of an Operating Licence granted either by the Gambling Commission or by the Local Authority or it is an exempt lottery by virtue of s.258 Gambling Act 2005 (and Schedule 11). It is very important to understand the difference between a lottery and a prize competition, as the latter can be operated free from regulation and statutory control. The distinction between a prize competition and a lottery is at times minimal and open to different interpretation. However, it is a distinction that must be understood by operators as those who promote illegal lotteries could be prosecuted.

The distinction is set out in s.14(5) of the 2005 Act. Section 14(5) states that a process which requires persons to exercise skill or judgement or to display knowledge shall be treated for the purpose of this section as relying wholly on chance if:

(a) The requirement cannot reasonably be expected to prevent a significant proportion of persons who participate in the arrangement of which the process forms part from receiving a prize and
(b) The requirement cannot reasonably be expected to prevent a significant proportion of the persons who wish to participate in that arrangement from doing so.

The section sets out to define a competition by specifying the circumstances in which the process will not be a competition and will be an illegal lottery which relies on chance. The Section states that to be a prize competition and free from regulatory control the process must be difficult enough so as to deter a significant proportion of persons from entering (s.14(5)(b)) and must be difficult enough to ensure that of those who are able to enter a significant proportion are prevented from winning (s.14(5)(a)).

The successful winner of a competition must succeed because of their skill and/or knowledge whereas the winner of a lottery will be determined by chance. Certain processes purport to have an element of skill and an element of chance in them and it is those processes which are difficult to interpret and upon which advice will have to be sought.

There have been many ingenious schemes to ensure that the process is a prize competition and free from regulatory control and not a lottery and the Gambling Commission have made it clear that advice will not be given on individual schemes. The Gambling Commission's position appears to be that no comment will be made on any scheme until it is up and running and it is only at that stage that if the Gambling Commission believe that the process is an unlawful lottery a letter will be written to operators. The Gambling Commission have, however, issued guidelines which assist to a certain extent. A crossword puzzle or several multiple choice questions which have a degree of difficulty and the answer to which is not obvious or contained in the text may be classed as a competition, whereas a single question followed by a draw may be lottery. No guidance is given as to what constitutes a significant proportion but the authors' view is that a significant proportion must at least exceed 50%.

PROPERTY SALES BY "LOTTERY"

There have been several instances of attempted commercial property transactions avoiding the market in a time of economic downturn by instead seeking to sell a pub or other alcohol-licensed premises by way of a "lottery". Whether such competitions fall to be classed as a lottery (and would therefore be illegal unless the seller held an operating licence) will depend on the how the scheme caters for the provisions noted above about skill and knowledge compared to chance. The authors are aware of several aborted attempts to sell alcohol-licensed premises in this way, and operators considering this would be advised to seek legal advice at an early stage. The Gambling Commission does not approve of the practice.

THE DEFINITION OF "LOTTERY"

If you are not a prize competition then you will be running a lottery which you can only do if you have an Operating Licence or it is an exempt lottery. Section 14 of the Act specifies two different types of lotteries, namely a simple lottery and a complex lottery but for either one an Operating Licence is required.

An arrangement is a **simple** lottery if:

- persons are required to pay in order to participate in the arrangement
- in the course of the arrangement one or more prizes are allocated to one or more members of a class, and
- the prizes are allocated by a process which relies wholly on chance

An arrangement is a **complex** lottery if:

- persons are required to pay in order to participate in the arrangement

- in the course of the arrangement one or more prizes are allocated to one or more members of a class
- the prizes are allocated by a series of processes, and
- the first of those processes relies wholly on chance

If a lottery is to be held in the above terms, an operating licence is required as it is an offence to promote a lottery unless the person promoting the lottery holds an operating licence. "Promoting" in this sense has a wide meaning[102].

Alcohol-licensed premises operators will however, be glad to hear that there are several exceptions negating the operating licence requirement: **Customer Lotteries**; **Small Society Lotteries**; **Incidental Non-Commercial Lotteries**; and **Private Lotteries**.

CUSTOMER LOTTERIES

The Act creates a new scheme which is permitted without a licence known as a customer lottery. The promoter must occupy business premises, participants must be physically present at the premises, tickets must be in documentary form, no profits can be made and the lottery cannot be advertised. The lottery can only be run once in any seven day period and the maximum prize is £50.

The following must also be observed:

- Tickets may only be sold by the promoter or his representative
- No rollovers are permitted
- Each ticket must state: the name and address of the promoter of the lottery; the class of persons who can purchase the tickets (i.e. the status of the customer); and that the right in a ticket is not transferable

102 The definition of "promoting a lottery" is to be found in s.252 of the 2005 Act.

A good example of this type of lottery is the 'Bonus Ball' where a sheet numbered 1 to 49 is made available and it would cost £1 to buy a number. If that number corresponds with the Bonus Ball from the next National Lottery draw the lucky person pockets £49 if all numbers have been sold. Note that, because the maximum prize in a 7 day period is £49, the "bonus ball" can only be run once a week – perhaps on the Saturday draw instead of the Wednesday draw; or vice versa.

SMALL SOCIETY LOTTERIES

Many country clubs and similar premises will be used to providing small lotteries for their members under the annual registration of the Lotteries & Amusements Act 1976. Under Schedule 11, Part 4 of the 2005 Act, an exemption is provided for "Small Society Lotteries", which are the equivalent provision to the 1976 registration. The society needs to be a non-commercial society in order for this part to apply[103]. The exemption from the need to apply for a lottery operating licence also applies to a remote gambling operating licence where ticket sales are made by means of remote communication.

In order to take up the exemption under this part, the following is required:

- Registration with the relevant authority[104] under Schedule 11 Part 5 (see below)
- The lottery must be promoted wholly on behalf of a non-commercial society
- The proceeds of the lottery may not exceed £20,000
- The annual proceeds of all lotteries may not exceed £250,000

---

103 "Non-commercial society" is defined under s.19 of the Act as a society conducted for charitable purposes, or in order to support sporting or cultural activities.

104 That is, the licensing authority.

- The lottery may be promoted for any of the purposes for which the promoting society is conducted
- At least 20% of the proceeds must be "applied to a purpose" for which the society is conducted
- Rollovers are permitted as long as the above maximum limits are observed
- The ticket must identify the society, the price, the name and address of a person of responsibility for the lottery, the date of the draw
- Ticket price must be the same[105]

Considering the second of these requirements, the Gambling Commission have taken the step of issuing guidance on what type of operator may meet the definition of "non-commercial" in relation to sporting clubs. The Commission state that it is their view that sporting clubs "*fall within section 19(1)(b) and are therefore deemed non-commercial*"[106].

THE REGISTRATION PROCEDURE FOR SMALL SOCIETY LOTTERIES

In order to enjoy the benefits of the Small Society Lottery exemption, the society must register with the relevant authority under Schedule 11 Part 5 of the Act. The application form and fee are prescribed in the Small Society Lotteries (Registration of Non-Commercial Societies) Regulations 2007[107], which was laid before Parliament on 8th August 2007 and came into force on 1st September 2007.

105 Note that the £2 maximum which had to observed under the old 1976 Act has been removed so there is no restriction on ticket price.

106 See the Gambling Commission publication "Lottery Guidance for charity trading companies and sporting clubs", December 2007, Page 3. The Guidance also discusses whether a charity's trading company can be regarded as established and conducted for a "non-commercial" purpose.

107 SI 2007 2328.

The initial fee is £40 and the annual renewal fee £20 thereafter, which must be paid within the period of two months before the anniversary of the registration. For those societies registered under the old 1976 regime, that existing registration was automatically converted to a registration under the new regime on 1 September 2007 and the first annual fee under the new Act was payable by 1 January 2008[108]. Thereafter, the fee of £20 must be paid within the period of two months which ends immediately before each anniversary of the registration.

A "statement of matters", signed by two appointed members of the society, must be sent to the relevant local authority no later than three months after the draw was made. This statement consists of a series of information with which the authority can monitor and ensure the lottery meets the conditions of being a Small Society Lottery and includes:

- The general arrangements for the lottery (including dates of draw and release of prizes)
- The proceeds of the lottery[109]
- The cost of prizes provided
- Organisational costs
- Amounts applied to a purpose of the society
- General expenses

INCIDENTAL NON-COMMERCIAL LOTTERIES

This type of lottery is exempt from the need to apply for an operating licence or local authority registration under Part 1 of Schedule 11 and replaces the old s.3 and s.15 of the Lotteries & Amusements Act 1976. According

---

108 See DCMS "Gambling Act 2005 Transitional Arrangements" published June 2007, Pg 75; and The Gambling Act 2005 (Transitional Provisions) (No.2) Order SI 2007 1758.

109 s.254 defines "proceeds" as "the aggregate of amounts paid in respect of the purchase of lottery tickets".

to the Gambling Commission guidance document "Lotteries and the Law (Gambling Act 2005), issued in May 2007, an "Incidental Non-Commercial Lottery" is one that is incidental to a non-commercial event and is created to provide for such occasions as school fetes or dinner dances. The key question here is whether an event of this sort is commercial or not: if all monies raised in connection with the event go towards a purpose which is not for private gain, then it meets the definition of non-commercial. There are, however three conditions to the running of such lotteries:

- Deductions for expenses may be made. This amount is prescribed in The Gambling Act 2005 (Incidental Non-Commercial Lotteries) Regulations 2007[110] and the maximum deduction for prizes is £500. The maximum deduction for costs is £100
- The Lottery cannot be a rollover
- Tickets must be sold on the day of the event and the result made publicly while the event takes place

PRIVATE LOTTERIES

There are three types of so-called "private" lotteries exempt under Part 2 of Schedule 11 – private lotteries, work lotteries and residents' lotteries.

Private Lotteries: these can be conducted by societies such as clubs only where tickets are sold to members or staff and must be for a purpose associated with the society.

Work Lotteries: this covers staff only internal lotteries such as a Grand National Sweepstake – the promoter must work on the premises and only workers may purchase tickets[111]. All profits (less reasonable expenses)

---

110 SI 2007 2040.

111 "Premises" under Schedule 11 Part 2 11(a) means a single set of premises.

must be used for prizes.

Residents Lotteries: resident only, not for profit lotteries were the promoter and purchasers must reside in the same premises. There are specific requirements in relation to advertising[112] for private lotteries, restricting advertising of private lotteries to the society, work or residential premises[113]. Further, the tickets must show the name and address of the promoter and the price.

THE LOTTERY CODE OF PRACTICE

The general code of practice for holders of operating licences (discussed in Chapter 2 above) has a section dedicated to lotteries, but the four exceptions noted here do not have a specific code issued by the Gambling Commission. This is because regulation is left to the local authority, who can implement their own provisions for control under Part 11 of the Act.

FREE DRAWS

Draws with no participation or entry fee are exempt from statutory control. As with any form of gaming, betting, or participation in a lottery under the 2005 Act, it must be for money or "money's worth" to constitute gambling.

112 On advertising in general, see Chapter 13.
113 Schedule 11 Part 2 s.14. For the definition of "advertising" in this context, see Schedule 11 Part 7 s.61.

CHAPTER EIGHT
PRIZE GAMING

Operators of licensed premises should be aware of a type of event which sits between prize competitions and gaming and is known as "prize gaming".

The provisions of Part 13 of the 2005 Act relate to prize gaming. Prize gaming is defined under s.288 of the Act as gaming in which a prize exists that is not influenced by the number of players or the amount paid to participate. This can consist of a variety of types of games. With prize gaming, the "winnings" or "prize" is put up by the operator of the game in advance of the commencement of play and is therefore distinct from those forms of gambling where the stakes of participants make up the prize. The "prize" can be monetary or non-monetary.

The intention of "prize gaming" regulation is therefore aimed at covering low level gaming with "modest" participation fees and prizes, but remember that the participation fee cannot be used to provide any prize on offer. The intention is to stop gaming taking place where the prize is determined by the amount raised by participants.

Also, note that Paragraph 732 of the Explanatory Notes to the 2005 Act states: "*Section 288 does not prevent prizes being won in a way that depends on the progress or outcome of the game. This means that if different prizes can be claimed dependent on how quickly a win takes place (for example, calling "house" in a game of bingo within a certain number of calls), this is permitted.*"

Part 13 of the Act specifies how prize gaming can take place legally without an offence being committed under s.33 or s.37 of the 2005 Act (those relating to providing facilities for gambling or using premises for gambling). An offence is not committed under s.33 or s.37 if prize gaming is provided either on premises which have a Bingo Premises Licence or if the requirements of s.293 are met. The requirements of s.293 Gambling Act 2005 are:

- the facilities are provided in accordance with a Prize Gaming Permit granted under s.289(1) and schedule 14
- the facilities are provided as an Adult Gaming Centre or Licensed Family Entertainment Centre (s.292(1))
- the facilities for equal chance prize gaming are provided under the authority of a Family Entertainment Gaming Machine Permit (s.290(2)), or
- facilities for equal chance prize gaming are provided at a travelling fair as ancillary amusement (s.292)

The 2005 Act has regulated this area of gambling by creating a "Prize Gaming Permit", under s.289, which can be issued by a licensing authority and will apply if an operator wishes to offer such gaming, but who is not the holder of a premises licence or a Club Gaming Permit, as those permissions already allow this form of gaming. A Prize Gaming Permit does not permit the provision of machines, unless the machine is mechanised gambling equipment to provide, for example, low-level roulette. Further, there is a form of automatic entitlement to offer prize gaming in respect of adult gaming centres, family entertainment centres, bingo halls with bingo premises licences and travelling fairs, so long as four conditions can be met:

- Compliance with stake or participation fee limits as set down by The Gambling Act 2005 (Limits on Prize Gaming) Regulations 2007[114]. The limit is 50p per chance with an aggregate limit for all fees not to exceed £500
- The game must be played on one day and the result made known immediately
- The value of the prize must not exceed the prescribed amount, which under the aforementioned regulations is: a) where the prize is money, no more than £35 (or £50 in an Adult Gaming Centre) and b) the aggregate amount or value of prizes for which a game is played shall not exceed £500. This allows a number of prizes to be available in one game
- The participation must not be linked to other gambling

Children cannot participate in prize gaming unless it is equal chance prize gaming.

PRIZE GAMING PERMITS - APPLICATION PROCEDURE

The procedure for Prize gaming Permits is found in Schedule 14 to the 2005 Act. The applicant must be a person who "occupies" or "proposes to occupy", the premises to which the permit is to relate. This means that, in a leasehold situation, the tenant would be required to be the applicant. The application is made to the licensing authority in which locality the premises in question are wholly or partly located.

Before the licensing authority can grant an application for a Prize gaming Permit, they must consult the relevant chief constable[115], and they have the power under Paragraph 8 of Schedule 14 to have reference to a

114 SI 2007 1777.
115 Schedule 14 paragraph 10.

"statement of principles" which they can produce to use as a guide in determining such applications, for example, to have regard to the suitability of the applicant. Once issued, a permit lasts for 10 years and can be renewed, although there is no transfer facility.

The licensing authority does not need to have regard to the licensing objectives but it must take account of the Gambling Commission Guidance issued to Local Authorities under s.25 Gambling Act 2005. No conditions can be attached to the permit and the application cannot be refused until the applicant has been notified that that is what the licensing authority intends to do and the applicant has had the opportunity to make representations. Reasons must be given for any refusal. A Prize Gaming Permit, once granted, can be surrendered by the holder or forfeited by a court and it will also lapse if the holder ceases to occupy the premises and in other circumstances, for example, if the holder dies, becomes bankrupt or is incapable, mentally or physically, of carrying on.

If an application for a Prize Gaming Permit is refused, then the applicant can appeal to the Magistrates' Court for the area in question, as long as an appeal is submitted within 21 days of receipt of the notice of refusal.

PRIZE GAMING PERMITS – FEES

The fee for a Prize Gaming Permit is £300, however existing operators were permitted to make an application at a reduced £100 if the application was lodged prior to 1st September 2007. There is no annual fee.

THE PRIZE GAMING PERMIT CODE OF PRACTICE

There is no Code of Practice issued by The Gambling Commission in relation to this particular form of gaming, as the matter has been left to individual licensing authorities to deliberate. In accordance with the general provisions of the Act, licensing authorities will be required to produce a 3 yearly licensing policy statement. However, the Commission's guidance to Licensing Authorities states:

> "*In particular* [licensing authorities] *may want to set out the matters that they will take into account in determining the suitability of the applicant. Given that the premises will particularly appeal to children and young persons, in considering what to take into account in the application process and what information to request from the applicant, licensing authorities will want to give weight to child protection issues. Licensing authorities should as the applicant to set out the types of gaming that he or she is intending to offer and the applicant should be able to demonstrate that:*

- they understand the limits and prizes that are set out in regulations
- the gaming offered is within the law".

CHAPTER NINE
FAMILY ENTERTAINMENT CENTRES & ADULT GAMING CENTRES

The 2005 Act has identified two special types of premises called "Family Entertainment Centres" (FECs) (licensed and unlicensed) and "Adult Gaming Centres" (AGCs).The definition of the first of these is as follows:

Licensed Family Entertainment Centre: a premises in respect of which a family entertainment centre premises licence has effect[116]. This type of premises may offer Category C and D machines but will require an operating licence and a premises licence in order to do so.

(Unlicensed) Family Entertainment Centre: a premises other than an adult gaming centre wholly or mainly used for making gaming machines available for use[117]. This type of premises may only operate Category D machines, by way of a special machine permit called a Family Entertainment Centre Gaming Machine Permit under s.247 and Schedule 10 (discussed below).There is no requirement for an operating or premises licence. This type of regulation is aimed toward places such as seaside resorts, airports or motorway service centres, which offer a multitude of lower jackpot gaming machines, one-armed bandits, coin pushers and so on, and recognises that such premises are often frequented by families. In the result, this provision allows Category D machines to be provided, which have no age limit on use, so long as the relevant permit is in place.

116 s.238.
117 Ibid.,

Adult Gaming Centre: An AGC is premises in respect of which an adult gaming centre premises licence has effect[118]. Adult Gaming Centres may provide up to a total of 4 Category B3/B4 machines (i.e. those with larger jackpots), as well as an unlimited number of Category C and D machines, only where the appropriate operating licence and premises licence is in place. The consumption of alcohol on such premises is specifically prohibited. The use of this type of premises is restricted to over 18s only and children are not allowed in any part of the premises. A notice must be displayed to that effect, along with a notice confirming the prohibition of alcohol which applies to these premises[119]. The best example of an AGC premises is a high street arcade.

THE PROHIBITION OF ALCOHOL IN FECS AND AGCS

Before assessing the impact of these new creations on pubs and clubs, it must be acknowledged from the outset that there is an in-built difficulty in this area, and that is that under the Gambling Act 2005 (Mandatory and Default Conditions) Regulations 2007[120] the following condition applies on both FEC & AGC premises:

> *"No Alcohol shall be sold, or permitted to be consumed, at any time during which facilities for gambling are being provided on the premises"*

Why then, discuss FECs and AGCs in this area? The reason is that the matter does become live where existing operators with premises such as bowling alleys or snooker halls wish to create a special AGC or FEC area to take advantage of the higher jackpot machines that such a permission would allow.

---

118 s.237.
119 See the Commission's "Guidance to Licensing Authorities" 2nd Ed., June 2007 Page 131 paragraph 21.8.
120 SSI 2007 266.

UNLICENSED FECs AND THE PROHIBITION OF ALCOHOL

Unlike the FEC and AGC there is no similar obstruction on alcohol in respect of an unlicensed FEC, however it seems that there are some authorities having difficulty with this particular provision (or lack thereof) and are seeking to impose such a restriction in other ways – for example, by having it as part of their Statement of Principles.

FEC GAMING MACHINE PERMIT – APPLICATION PROCEDURE

An applicant for a FEC gaming machine permit must be, or proposes to become, the occupier of the relevant premises, in other words, a premises **not** holding an FEC premises licence[121]. The application is dealt with by the local licensing authority, which also sets out the form of application and direction on any supporting information/documentation which may, for example, include a plan showing location of machines. The applications may be delegated. The licensing authority may prepare a "statement of principles" as a guide to the exercise of their functions in processing such applications.

Once an application has been received, the authority must consult the police, and then either grant or refuse the application – they do not have the power to attach conditions. The permit has a lifespan of 10 years but may be renewed (at the same fee – see below). There is no transfer facility afforded under Schedule 10 of the Act, so a new operator would need to apply for a new grant. There is no limit on the number of D machines that may be provided once this type of permit is in place.

121 This type of permit can only be applied for by an unlicensed family entertainment centre. The FEC premises licence allows the use of C and D machines without a further permit.

FEC GAMING MACHINE PERMIT – FEES

The administration of the fee has been set by The Gambling Act 2005 (Family Entertainment Centre Gaming Machine) (Permits) Regulations 2005[122], which came into force on 21 May 2007. The fee for a new permit (or subsequent renewal) is £300, however existing operators[123] were allowed to submit applications with a fee of £100 prior to 1 September 2007. There is no annual fee but a replacement copy licence attracts a fee of £15.

FECs AND ALCOHOL-LICENSED PREMISES

Unfortunately, this rather complicated area of the interplay between gambling and licensing law does not end there. Notwithstanding the prevention on the sale of alcohol, there is some debate over whether an alcohol-licensed premises could also be an FEC, especially for premises such as bowling alleys, most of which hold an alcohol licence[124] but also have areas set aside to provide arcade and gaming machines. This further dilemma is grounded in the possibility of applying for two conflicting types of machine permit: an FEC gaming machine permit, and a Licensed Premises Gaming Machine Permit.

The answer should be based on the number of machines to be provided. If the premises are not **wholly or mainly** used for providing machines, then the machines that are provided may continue to be so by virtue of the Licensed Premises Gaming Machine permit route (or the automatic entitlement procedure if two or less machines), open to alcohol-licensed premises. This means that bowling alley operators who had been providing machines under s.34 of the Gaming Act 1968 may continue to do so without any worry about "double licensing" (so long as they have, of

122 SI 2007 454.
123 In other words, those who provide machines by way of s.34 of The Gaming Act 1968.
124 Typically an entertainment licence under the Licensing (Scotland) Act 1976, but a premises licence under The Licensing (Scotland) Act 2005.

course, gained a Licensed Premises Gaming Machine Permit or automatic entitlement). However, if the number of machines is such that they are the main facility being provided then it is likely an FEC licence is required where those machines are category C or above; or if only category D machines a FEC machine permit. Whether or not a premises is "wholly or mainly used" for the provision of machines will be a matter for the local authority.

The Ariadne's thread for this maze will depend on whether the operator has attempted to "de-licence" an area in order to take advantage of higher machines for that area by applying for an FEC or an AGC. In that case, the premises could very well hold both an FEC gaming machine permit, and a Licensed Premises Gaming Machine Permit – one relating to the separate FEC area and the other relating to those machines in the bar or otherwise in the premises but not within the separate area.

ACCESS BETWEEN ARCADES AND OTHER LICENSED AREAS

A further difficulty is access between separately licensed areas within the same premises. In our example, say an entertainment facility provides one or two bowling lanes but the main provision is machines. The premises also has bar facilities. The arcade section of the premises would be required to hold an FEC and the bar would of course be covered by an alcohol licence (which may have its own machines as discussed above). There are access restrictions regarding intercommunication between licences in The Gambling Act 2005 (Mandatory and Default Conditions) (England & Wales) Regulations 2007[125] – but subsequent guidance from the Gambling Commission has confirmed that this condition does not apply between FEC and alcohol-licensed premises[126].

In any event, there must have been substantial consternation from

125 SI 2007 1409, Schedules 3 and 4.

126 For further discussion on this issue, see the Gambling Commission's publication "Guidance to Licensing Authorities", 2nd Edition, June 2007: Pg 65.

operators of such premises disagreeing with local authority decisions on licensing and access because the Gambling Commission took the step of issuing a statement on individual applications called "Access between Arcades" on 11 July 2007, in which they stress that they do not have jurisdiction to deliberate on specific cases, nor do they have the power to overturn the decisions of local authorities.

SPLIT PREMISES AND "PRIMARY ACTIVITY"

Since the 2005 Act came into force, there have been several examples of operators seeking to "split" their premises so that two gambling premises licences would be required for each of the "areas" in the premises. The primary reason for this separation is to double the numbers of machines which may be made available – with two licences for a premises, the maximum number for each licence could be observed and therefore twice the number of machines could be provided than if the premises had one licence.

There has been some controversy over using this route. The Gambling Commission has expressed concern that operators are somehow using a "loophole" to double machines and that the premises itself is not genuinely separated. The question of "primary activity" comes into play here as if there are a high number of machines so that the use of machines outweighs the provision of other forms of gambling, this may fall foul of s.150 of the Act, which, the Commission says, is structured in such a way that a premises licence authorising a primary activity should not be used to provide, primarily, anther form of gambling activity.

If the machines do not become the primary activity the there should be no issue. The process here is effectively having two new premises licence applications processed where only one had existed before. Licensing authorities concerned about this should note that the 2005 Act defines a "premises" as "any place"[127], which means that is perfectly competent for a single building to have more than one gambling premises licence, so long as the licences do not overlap.

The difficulty then, may arise when considering in what ways premises are "split" and how the separation of separately licensed areas may be managed. The matter was considered in *Leisure (UK) Ltd v London Borough of Islington*[128] in which the local authority successfully defended its decision to refuse premises licence applications which sought to subdivide an existing adult gaming centre to increase the number of machines available. Taking into account the new Gambling Commission guidance, the district judge ruled that in this case the "artificial division" of the premises into three units "would not create three premises". The judge also said that a broad interpretation of "artificial" should be considered in relation to whether premises are genuinely separate and not just physically separate. An earlier unreported case adds to the debate, namely *Luxury Leisure v South Tyneside Council*[129]. Again an operator split premises, but in this case with the admitted intention of hoping to use an entitlement to further machines. The Judge held that the test should be whether the proposed split would "create objectively recognisable separate places". Significantly, he also said that although the proposals in the instant case did not meet his test, he did not see why an alternative reconfiguration of the existing premises might result in a successful "split". It would seem that each proposal to "split" should be taken on its own merits.

---

127 s.152.
128 26 May 2009, unreported.
129 24th July 2008, unreported.

LICENSED FAMILY ENTERTAINMENT CENTRE CODE OF PRACTICE[130]

The Code of Practice was released in August 2007 in a document which also contained a list of suggested examples for conditions which would be applicable to a licensed FEC. The Code of Practice is primarily based around social responsibility and protection of children. The following items are representative of the code:

- The Licensee must have policies and procedures to promote socially responsible gambling
- The Licensee must have policies and procedures to prevent underage gambling
- The Licensee must make information on how to deal with problem gambling available

UNLICENSED FAMILY ENTERTAINMENT CENTRE CODE OF PRACTICE

- There is no code of practice as such for an **unlicensed** FEC, and even where that type of premises seeks to provide category D gaming machines by way of an FEC permit, this type of gambling is probably the least regulated and monitored under the 2005 Act.

ADULT GAMING CENTRE CODE OF PRACTICE

This was issued alongside the FEC code in August 2007 and the provisions are virtually the same as those noted above. There is however a series of varying typical licence conditions for this type of venue and the reader is directed to the Gambling Commission's website for more information.

---

130 There is no code of practice for unlicensed FECs – the regulation is to be found in the local authorities "statement of principles", discussed above at footnote 21.

CHAPTER TEN
BINGO

Bingo is a form of equal chance gaming permitted on alcohol-licensed premises, but as there are specific provisions for forms of low-level activity bingo in clubs and alcohol-licensed premises under Part 12 of the Act, and because bingo is often considered separately in the national consciousness, so it is dealt with separately here. "Bingo" is identified in the Act only as "*any version of that game irrespective of by what name it is described*"[131]. In the annotations to the Current Law Statutes of the 2005 Act, by Carl Rohsler, the author provides a more useful definition: "*a social game of chance (having the characteristics also of a lottery) where players seek to match a series of numbers drawn at random against a further set of numbers which have been pre-selected for them in the hope of winning a prize*"[132].

Under the Act, clubs and pubs can offer bingo without a permit or licence provided that:

- No sums are deducted from sums staked or won – so there can be no "rake" from the prize pot
- No participation fee is charged in respect of bingo games in pubs and the participation fee is no more than £1 per person per day in respect of bingo games in clubs, or £3 where a club gaming permit is held

---

131 Section 353(1).
132 Rhosler, Carl (2005) "The Gambling Act 2005", Thomson Sweet & Maxwell: Pg 253.

- Games are held on the premises
- Games are not linked with games held on other premises, and
- There is a maximum stake per game per player of £5 for bingo in pubs[133].

Further, s.281 of the 2005 Act disapplies "high turnover" bingo from a "high turnover" period from the general exemption for such gaming under s.279. Put shortly, this means alcohol-licensed premises may operate bingo so long as the aggregate stakes or prizes are not in excess of £2000 in any seven day period[134]. If this maximum is breached, and the operator intends to carry out the same level of bingo again within the following twelve months, then this will move them into the category of "high turnover" mentioned above and activate the requirement for an operating licence[135].

In order to provide bingo facilities, there are five conditions to be met under s.279:

- That the provision of the bingo satisfies the limits as laid down by regulations in relation to the amount of a stake and the amount of a prize
- No levy or other amount may be deducted from the stakes made by players or from winnings received
- There can be no participation fee
- Bingo facilities provided on one premises may not "link" to games in

---

133 Gambling Commission's "Advice on Gaming in Clubs and Alcohol-licensed Premises", September 2008: Page 7 para 9.1.

134 The local authority must inform the Commission if there is evidence this maximum is not being adhered to. See the Commission's "Guidance to Licensing Authorities" 2nd Ed., June 2007 Page 104 paragraph 18.10.

135 Although not a premises licence, so long as the terms of the Act have been followed: see Gambling Commission publication "Advice on Gaming in Clubs and Alcohol-licensed Premises", September 2008: Page 8 para 9.3.

other premises[136]

- Children[137] and young persons[138] are excluded from participation

The Equal Chance Gaming On Alcohol-licensed Premises Code Of Practice applies in short measure here, imposing a solitary duty on the "gaming supervisor" (the premises manager) in respect of bingo games as follows:

- If the total stakes or prizes exceed £2000 in any seven day period the gaming supervisor must contact the Commission

Member's clubs and miner's welfare institutes can only offer bingo to members or their *bona fide* guests.

136 This is no doubt to differentiate bingo from proper bingo halls, where country wide "superdraws" can be played, where players from all over the UK are participating in a single, simultaneous game – the attraction being, of course, higher winnings.

137 "Children" means persons aged 15 and under (Section 45(1)).

138 "Young persons" means persons aged 16 or 17(Section 45(2)).

CHAPTER ELEVEN
REMOTE GAMBLING

In recent years there has been a phenomenal growth of gambling in situations where the person gambling is not situated in or at the same premises as the gaming equipment. The most common form of gambling of this kind is via the internet or via a telephone. As the industry continues to develop new technology and the public responds positively to new innovations (Blackberries, Smart-phones, I-phones and so on), so operators must take great care to ensure that the regulations set out in the 2005 Act are not breached.

Remote gambling by very definition is difficult to regulate. The difficulties for the Regulator are connected to the facts that the server which supplied the gaming website may be situated in one jurisdiction, the game itself may be played on a piece of equipment which was designed in another jurisdiction and the game may be played by a player who is in another jurisdiction. An example of this would be a person gaming on the internet in a bar in London on a computer which was made in Germany and on a gaming website which is based in Gibraltar.

Regulation applies equally to the location in which the server is positioned (Gibraltar in the above example) as it does to the location in which the electronic device through which gambling takes place is positioned (London in the example).

Remote gambling is defined in s.4 of the Act as gambling by means of remote communication, including the internet, telephone, television, radio or any other technology which can facilitate communication, and there is a provision for a remote operating licence under s.67[139]. There are now quiz and gaming machines available that can connect to the internet; and of course some alcohol-licensed premises and clubs provide internet access facilities through computers to the public or more commonly Wi-Fi access.

Section 5 of the 2005 Act defines "facilities for gambling". A person provides such facilities if he invites others to gamble in accordance with arrangements made by him, provides, operates or administers arrangements for gambling or participates in the operation or administration of gambling by others. Section 5(3) confirms that facilities for gambling are provided if facilities for remote communication are made available and the facilities are adapted or presented in such a way as to facilitate or draw attention to the possibility of their use for gambling and the nature, adaptation or presentation is such that (i) they cannot reasonably be expected to be used for purposes other than gaming or (ii) they are intended to be used wholly or mainly for gambling.

Gambling means playing of a game of chance for a prize although the definition also could include games which involve both an element of skill and chance and again the Secretary of State may provide that a specified activity is or is not gaming under the act (Section 6(6)). Other chapters in this book deal specifically with the provision of gaming machines on licensed premises which fall into various categories which define the sort of machine that different alcohol-licensed premises may operate. In this chapter we

139 For more information on the tax implications of remote gambling, and how the 2005 Act deals with remote gambling provided by other legal jurisdictions, see "Remote Gambling – all bets off?" The Journal, September 2007, pp 32 – 33.
http://www.journalonline.co.uk/article/1004509.aspx.

concentrate on the provision of an electronic device, for example the internet, on licensed premises upon which remote gambling can take place.

If you provide online licensed premises a computer or other electronic device upon which people can access gambling websites, then you may require a licence, otherwise you would commit an offence. Whether or not you are committing an offence depends on whether or not your computer or electronic device falls into the category of a gaming machine. Under s.235(2)(a) of the Act a computer is not a "gaming machine" simply by virtue of the fact that it can be used to participate in remote gambling, but that exemption only applies where the computer is for domestic or "dual-use" (publicly available) computers. The intention here is, of course, to exempt PCs with internet access that are not specifically configured for gambling activities, but how does this affect alcohol-licensed premises?

The answer is be found by looking at the definitions of "domestic" and "dual use" computer, contained in the Gambling Act 2005 (Gaming Machines) (Definitions) Regulations 2007[140]. A **domestic computer** is a computer that is:

- capable of being used for a purpose that is not related to gambling
- is located in a private dwelling
- if used, is used on a domestic occasion

A **dual-use computer** is a computer that is capable of being used for a purpose that is not related to gambling and either i)is not knowingly adapted in such a way as to facilitate, or to draw attention to the possibility of its use for gambling, or ii) it is so adapted but only where:

- The use is restricted to, or intended to be restricted to, private use

140 SI 2007 2082, which came into force on 1st September 2007.

- It is being adapted, repaired or maintained and would otherwise be restricted to private use and enabling the computer for gambling is not the purpose of the adaptation, repair or maintenance

So that, the first definition of dual use computer seems to neatly provide an exemption for the provision of internet facilities in hotel rooms, but if a computer was specifically set up for gambling (perhaps by linking to an online site) in, for example, a snooker hall, then it would fall to be considered as a gaming machine.

This is the key issue insofar as operators of alcohol-licensed premises are concerned. It is not possible without a licence under the Gambling Act 2005 to provide in alcohol-licensed premises a computer which only has access to a gaming site. It is also not possible to provide a computer which is marketed in a way so as to direct customers to a particular gaming site or, indeed, to persuade customers to go to a gaming website. There is, however, nothing in the legislation which prevents computers being provided in alcohol-licensed premises and upon which customers can gamble if they so choose, as long as those customers have access to all other sites and are not directed to the gaming website.

If an operator wishes to provide a form of gambling both remotely and non-remotely, both a remote and non-remote operating licence would be required. In other words, an alcohol-licensed premises which does not otherwise require an operating licence may well be caught if they are providing computers with internet access, set up for the provision of online gambling.

For those operators who do supply machines on their premises capable of allowing gambling via an internet connection, there is now further guidance available from the Commission on what may or may not constitute "remote gambling equipment", including a discussion on marketing of bonuses and other incentives to customers in the form of options to gamble, client application download servers, as well as a list of the technical components which by definition under s.36(4) of the 2005 Act, would fall to be classed as remote gambling equipment[141].

The Gambling Commission publishes quarterly surveys on participation levels in Remote Gambling. The June 2007 survey showed that approximately 8.6 per cent of the population gamble remotely; by the release of the December 2007 survey this figure has risen to 9.1%.These findings seem remarkably small given that in recent estimates two thirds of the British population are now "on line", and this figure is likely to rise as more facilities become available and technology advances.

If the operator of an alcohol-licensed premises wishes to apply for an operating licence under the 2005 Act then the application is made to the Gambling Commission in the usual way. There are specific rules for remote operating licences, set out in s.89, which gives wide ranging powers to the Gambling Commission in respect of remote operating licences, which include powers to establish standards, to attach conditions and to make arrangements for the administration of tests amongst other things.

Once an operator has been granted an operating licence then the licence conditions and codes of practice must be complied with so as to support the objectives of the Act and one of the general codes which must be followed by all remote operators is that gambling on websites must display information which can be seen before any gambling takes place, confirming that the operator is regulated by the Gambling Commission and displaying their licence number and a link to the Gambling Commission website.

141 The interested reader is directed to the Gambling Commission publication "Remote Gambling: Advice Note", March 2008; http://tinyurl.com/29oa5d.

CHAPTER TWELVE
TEMPORARY USE NOTICES

Part 9 of the Gambling Act 2005 has created a *sui generis* provision which, upon reading s.215 of the Act, would seem to enable alcohol-licensed premises to be used for the purposes of gambling in relation to a short-term special event of some description, known as a "Temporary Use Notice" under s.33 of the Licensing Act 2003.

A Temporary Use Notice essentially gives a person who holds an operating licence permission to use a premises unlicensed in respect of the Gambling Act 2005 to provide gambling facilities, in connection with a special, temporary gambling event of some nature.

Consultation has made it clear that alcohol-licensed premises had been specifically thought of as a premises for which a Temporary Use Notice could apply: "*The Department* [DCMS] *has taken the view that a Notice should be used to provide premises such as Hotels to provide equal chance gaming tournaments*". The consultation offered no further guidance on what sort of event could be used for a Temporary Use Notice so it would appear that is the sole *intended* use for them, however the Commission has said: "*Premises which may be suitable for a temporary use notice would include hotels, conference centres and sporting venues*"[142].

142 "Guidance to Licensing Authorities" 2nd Edition, June 2007: Page 81 paragraph 14.1.

The Gambling Act 2005 (Temporary Use Notices) Regulations 2007[143] outline that the "activities which may be specified" in an a temporary use notice are for any form of equal chance gaming (except equal chance gaming by way of gaming machines), where those participating in the gaming are taking part in a larger competition which has been designed in such a way so that the event will produce a single, overall winner. A practical example of this sort of event could be a national poker event, with "heats" leading up to a final.

TEMPORARY USE NOTICE - APPLICATION PROCEDURE

A premises may not be subject to a Temporary Use Notice for more than any 21 days in a period of 12 months. That could be 21 one day Notices, or one 21 day Notice, or any combination totalling 21 days. The notice itself is in a prescribed form which is laid down in the regulations - which came into force on 1 December 2007 – and the fee in England & Wales is anything up to a maximum of £500, to be set by the relevant licensing authority[144].

The Temporary Use Notice must be lodged with the relevant licensing authority, with a copy sent to the Gambling Commission, the relevant Chief Constable, and HM Customs, a full 3 months prior to the 1st date on which the Notice is sought to take effect. There is a separate notice to be completed if the premises to which the notice is attached is a vessel.

Any of the consulted parties mentioned above may make representations to the Notice having regard to the licensing objectives. Any objection must be lodged with both the applicant and the relevant licensing authority not later than 14 days after the date the Notice was received. There are powers of inspection conferred on a police constable, and enforcement

143 SI 2007 3157.
144 The fee in Scotland is a standard £350.

officer or authorised person under s.315, specifically in relation to Notices, to assess the "likely effects" of the granting of the Notice.

The key point is that temporary use notices may only be applied for by persons holding an operating licence under the Gambling Act 2005, so a normal alcohol licence holder cannot himself pursue such an activity for his premises unless he has made arrangements with an operating licence holder. An example of how this could work in practice is where a national casino chain could reach an agreement with a hotel to use the temporary use notice procedure to have gaming events in that hotel.

CHAPTER THIRTEEN
ADVERTISING

If an alcohol-licensed premises operator wishes to take advantage of any of the new abilities to have gambling as discussed in this book, he must also be aware of the provisions in relation to the advertising of such events. Historically, it is reasonable to promulgate the view that advertising and gambling were not exactly cheery bedfellows and operators were, for several years, in the unprivileged position of being a *persona non grata*.

Previously gambling premises existed, but could not advertise the fact. Until 25 years ago it was the case that bookmakers' offices were, to passers by, places of mystique – forbidden dens behind frosted glass, usually in the back streets. The reasoning behind this was to prevent any unnecessary "stimulation" of gambling in the population at large, who would, no doubt, become corrupted by glancing in at the environs of the traditional bookmakers' premises[145].

This antediluvian approach had been eroded during the de-regulation of the previous legislation and has been eradicated under the new Act. The Gambling Act has reformed the rules on gambling advertising which had been inconsistent across different sectors. For example bookmakers were allowed to advertise in papers but casinos were not. Part 16 of the Act effectively allows advertising for any form of gambling, with three general

145 For an interesting précis of gambling and advertising, see Carl Rohsler's notes to s.16 of the Act.

exceptions which may affect operators of alcohol-licensed premises:

- Section 328(4) provides that the form of advertisements has to have regard to the need to protect children and other vulnerable persons from being harmed or exploited by gambling. Contravention is an offence that can lead to 51 weeks imprisonment[146].
- It is also an offence to advertise a form of gambling not open for use by an alcohol-licensed premises[147].
- Section 331 makes it an offence to advertise non-EEA gambling. Foreign gambling is gambling which either physically takes place in a non-EEA state[148], or gambling by remote means which is not regulated by the gambling law of any EEA state[149]. It should also be noted that for the purposes of this section, Gibraltar is treated as if it is an EEA state.

Any advertising of gambling facilities is subject to two codes: the CAP (Committee of Advertising Practice) and BCAP (Broadcast Committee of Advertising Practice), and are in place to ensure that any advertising of such facilities cannot harm or exploit children or vulnerable persons. CAP covers non-broadcast advertising, and BCAP covers broadcast advertising[150].

Operators wishing to advertise gambling facilities should ensure that they comply with the CAP or BCAP code as appropriate. Details of these organisations can be found in Appendix B.

---

146 S. 328(7).
147 s. 330.
148 European Economic Area.
149 For a discussion on the special rules surrounding online advertising, see Coles, Tony & Nocton, Nick (2006) "Online Gambling Advertising in the UK", Casino Lawyer, Vol 2 No 3 Summer 2006, pg 10 – 11. http://www.gaminglawmasters.com/casinolawyer/CL0706.pdf.
150 For further information on this, see the Gambling Commission publication "Guide to Advertising Codes", October 2007.

There is also a separate "Gambling Industry Code for Socially Responsible Gambling". This voluntary code introduces further standards created to protect children and vulnerable persons over and above the CAP and BCAP Advertising Codes. This code has been agreed by the Government and includes a number of measures requested by the Secretary of State for Culture, Media and Sport[151].

The report of the Advertising Standards Authority from 2007, which was published in February 2008, stated that there was a total of 784 adverts monitored by ASA - and only 1% appeared to be in breach. Director General of ASA, Christopher Graham, said: "*The results of this compliance survey are confirmation that advertising self-regulation is working effectively and that advertisers in the gambling sector are demonstrating a proper concern for social responsibility in their marketing communications*".

At the time of writing, the Gambling Commission announced that they are still seeking balance between the ability to advertise and ensuring that it is not abused. Several internet operations and some of the large bookmakers have already been told to remove certain adverts, due to their infringement of the minimum standards necessary for advertising. There is the potential for leasing of advertisements for gambling and it is therefore important that licensed premises operators do not fall foul of them, should they be offering legitimate gambling facilities at their venues.

151 For further information see the publication "Gambling Industry Code for Socially Responsible Gaming", August 2007. The DCMS also produced an "Advertising Fact Pack" and an "Advertising Media Fact Pack", August 2007.

CHAPTER FOURTEEN
SUPERVISION & COMPLIANCE

The Gambling Commission has the power to appoint Compliance Officers[152], whose general role is to monitor and advise persons offering gambling in respect of their duties under the 2005 Act, and to ensure that the objectives are upheld. In a written answer on 25 February 2008, Gerry Sutcliffe (then Parliamentary Under-Secretary, DCMS), said in response to a question on the "manpower" of the enforcement arm of the Commission:

> *"The Gambling Commission has 55 regionally based compliance staff (all of whom are designated as enforcement officers). In addition there is a specialist enforcement team of 10 officers based in Birmingham with national responsibilities. There are eight further specialist compliance staff (sector experts/technical advisers) who are also appointed as enforcement officers. Three compliance officers and one enforcement officer have been appointed since the Gambling Act 2005 came into force on 1 September 2007."*

The Compliance Officers have the right to enter and inspect premises if they suspect that gambling other than private and non-commercial gaming is occurring, and request to see relevant documentation[153].

There are specific provisions for the right of entry in relation to alcohol-

152 S.303.
153 S.307.

licensed premises and clubs. In respect of licensed premises[154], the Compliance Officer or other local authority officer[155] may enter premises with a licence for *on-sales* for the following purposes:

- determining that the equal chance gaming limits (e.g. poker) are being observed
- ensuring that any bingo complies with the relevant limits
- ascertaining the number and category of gaming machines being made available

In relation to club premises, the power of a relevant local authority officer to inspect is limited to investigating premises in connection with the consideration of an application for a Club Gaming or Club Machine Permit, however a police constable and Compliance Officers have an ongoing right of inspection to determine whether gaming is taking place in accordance with[156]:

- The exempt gaming provisions under s.269
- A Club Gaming Permit
- A Club Machine Permit

The Gambling Compliance Officers, relevant local authority officers and police also have rights of entry and inspection in relation to premises with Prize Gaming Permits[157], Temporary Use Notices[158], Registered Small Society Lottery providers[159] and Family Entertainment Centres[160]. These powers also extend to premises licences, and indeed premises on

154 S.310.
155 No doubt an alcohol licensing officer.
156 S.313.
157 S.311.
158 S.315.
159 S.314.
160 S.309.

which it is suspected that gaming or betting is taking place without the appropriate licence, permit or exemption.

For alcohol-licensed premises, this means ensuring that, for example, the poker, lottery and bingo limits are not breached, and that the gambling is being supervised in an effective way.

TEST PURCHASING OF AGE RESTRICTED GAMBLING ACTIVITIES

The 2005 Act permits the use of "test purchasing", where an authorised person[161] can send a young person to a premises in order to establish whether or not the operator is adhering to the rules regarding age restricted forms of gambling activity. This power extends to visits on alcohol-licensed premises to ensure no-one under age is permitted to use a Category C (or above) machine, and may also be used to check the age of entrants for poker and equal chance gaming is being observed.

Due to the overlap between the 2005 Act and the Licensing Act 2003, it is reasonable to presume that a certain amount of "partnership working" has evolved with the gambling compliance officers, local authority enforcement officers, and of course the police.

Operators of alcohol-licensed premises must be vigilant not only with "due diligence" steps to prevent under age alcohol sales, but also access by persons under 18 to gambling facilities such as gaming machines or equal chance gaming tournaments.

161 "Authorised person" here means a Gambling Commission compliance officer, a relevant local authority officer such as an alcohol enforcement officer, and the police.

CHAPTER FIFTEEN
THE LAST THROW

There are a number of other new provisions introduced by the 2005 Act that may be of some relevance.

GAMBLING CONTRACTS

For centuries "contracts" for gambling, for example a bookie's slip, have been deemed to be unenforceable (though not illegal) in Scots law, as the courts have viewed them as *sponsiones ludicrae*, a provision which the Scottish Government say dates back to 1780[162]. Section 335 of the Act abolishes the doctrine of *sponsiones ludicrae* and as of 1 September 2007 a gambling contract is enforceable in court.

QUIZ GAMING & SKILL COMPETITIONS

Pub quiz gurus will be delighted to hear that games with prizes that are based on knowledge, skill or judgement are exempted from regulation under s.14(5), although it is worth noting that under the Licensing (Scotland) Act 2005 any prize for a pub quiz of an alcoholic nature is likely to fall foul of the conditions prohibiting "irresponsible promotions". This exemption does, of course, extend to quiz machines that fall to be considered as a "Skill with Prizes" machine discussed in Chapter 4 above.

---

162 For a modern restatement of the doctrine, see Cumming v Mackie 1973 SC 728 and the more recent Ferguson v Littlewood Pools Ltd 1997 SLT 309.

Operators under the Licensing (Scotland) Act 2005 will wish to include reference to quiz nights and other entertainments of that nature in their operating plan.

CHAIN GIFTS/PYRAMID SCHEMES

Section 43 of the Act creates a new offence to invite someone to join or otherwise promote a chain scheme, unless they do so with the knowledge that that it such a scheme. It is not, however, an offence to join a chain scheme.

PRIVATE NON COMMERCIAL GAMING

Section 296 of the Act exempts private gaming or betting from any statutory control. This sort of question sometimes appears in relation to poker games in private hotel rooms. Such activities will fall under s.296 and therefore entirely legal.

CREDIT CARDS & GAMING MACHINES

Under s.245 it is an offence to supply, install or make available a gaming machine designed or adapted to permit money to be paid by means of a credit card. This has not previously been an issue as technology could not cater for such a thing, but now it is quite easy for machines to be made where one has to simply insert a credit card and gambling may commence. Such machines are in use in Las Vegas and no doubt elsewhere. There appears to be no provision prohibiting the "change" facility on some jackpot machines, whereby a machine user can insert a £5, £10 or £20 note into a specified slot in return for coins to the same value.

CHEATING

Card sharks and hucksters beware – under s.42 of the Act not only is it an offence to cheat at gambling, but now it also an offence to do anything for the purpose of enabling or assisting another person to cheat at gambling. The first known convictions under this section of the Act occurred in June 2009.

BETTING IN LICENSED PREMISES

The title of this book was chosen purposefully. Section 3 of the 2005 Act defines "gambling" as betting, gaming and participation in a lottery. Betting is entirely **illegal** on alcohol-licensed premises and clubs. The Gambling Commission has reinforced this by taking the step of producing a statement to that effect: "*No commercial betting at all, regardless of the level of stakes, is allowed in pubs and clubs. It is not socially responsible and those who provide betting in pubs and clubs – publicans, designated premises supervisors and club officials – are providing illegal facilities for gambling and are breaking the law*"[163].

There is nothing to spot a person from filling out his betting slip in an alcohol-licensed premises, or completing his football pools fixed odds coupon; but any bets must be placed by that person in the appropriate gambling establishment themselves – the bookie's "runner" is a thing of the past.

163 See the Gambling Commission publication "Betting in Pubs & Clubs", February 2008. Note that the Commission has elected to use the phrase "Designated Premises Supervisor", the English equivalent of the Section 11 nominee under the Licensing (Scotland) Act 1976 and the Premises Manager under the Licensing (Scotland) Act 2005.

APPENDIX A
A GUIDE TO RELEVANT TERMS IN THE ACT

"*advertising*" (s.327)
"*alcohol licence*" (s.277)
"*authorised person*" (s.304)
"*child*" (s.45)
"*club gaming permit*" (s.271)
"*club machine permit*" (s.273)
"*commercial club*" (s.267)
"*equal chance gaming*" (s.8)
"*exempt lottery*" (s.258)
"*family entertainment centre*" (s.238)
"*family entertainment centre gaming machine permit*" (s.247)
"*gambling*" (s.3)
"*gaming*" (s.6(1))
"*game of chance*" (s.6(2))
"*gaming machine*" (s.235)
"*licensing objectives*" (s.1)
"*licensed premises gaming machine permit*" (s.283)
"*lottery*" (s.14 and s.256)
"*lottery ticket*" (s.253)
"*members' club*" (s.266)
"*miner's welfare club*" (s.268)
"*non commercial gaming*" (s.297)
"*non-commercial society*" (s.19)
"*operating licence*" (Part 5)
"*participant*" (s.353)
"*participation fee*" (s.344)
"*personal licence*" (Part 6)
"*premises licence*" (Part 8)
"*private gaming*" (s.295 and Part 1 of Schedule 15)
"*prize*" (s.6)
"*prize*" in relation to gaming machines (s.239)
"*prize*" in relation to lotteries (s.14)
"*prize gaming permit*" (s.289)
"*proceeds*" (s.254)
"*profits*" in relation to lotteries (s.254)
"*profits*" in relation to non-commercial prize gaming (s.299)
"*remote gambling*" (s.4)
"*remote operating licence*" (s.67)
"*stake*" (s.353)
"*temporary use notice*" (s.215)
"*travelling fair*" (s.286)
"*winnings*" (s.353)
"*young person*" (s.45)

APPENDIX B
RELEVANT WEBSITES

LINKS TO THE REGULATORS

The Gambling Commission
www.gamblingcommission.gov.uk

Department of Media, Culture & Sport (Gambling Section)
www.culture.gov.uk/what_we_do/Gambling_racing

The Gambling Appeals Tribunal
www.gamblingappealstribunal.gov.uk

LINKS TO PROBLEM GAMBLING ORGANISATIONS

Gamcare
www.gamcare.co.uk

Gambler's Anonymous
www.gamblersanonymous.org.uk

LINKS TO OTHER USEFUL WEBSITES

British Institute of Innkeeping
www.bii.org.uk

The Institute of Licensing
www.iolf.org

The Lotteries Council
www.lotteriescouncil.org.uk/

The Jockey Club
www.thejockeyclub.co.uk/

The Office of Public Sector Information (OPSI)
www.opsi.gov.uk

Committee of Advertising Practice & Broadcast Committee of Advertising Practice
www.cap.org.uk

APPENDIX C
GUIDE TO RELEVANT REGULATIONS

This list of regulations is not exhaustive. The regulations can be viewed in full on the website of the Office of Public Sector Information (OPSI). The date provided is the date the regulations came into force unless otherwise specified.

THE ACT

The Gambling Act 2005 (C.19)
The Gambling Act gives effect to the government's proposals for reform of the law on gambling. The Act contained a new regulatory system to govern the provision of all gambling in Great Britain other then the national lottery and spread betting. The Act repealed the Betting, Gaming & Lotteries Act 1963, the Gaming Act 1968 and the Lotteries and Amusements Act 1976.
7 April 2005

Licensing Authority Policy Statement (First Appointed Day) Order 2006 SI 637
Section 349 of the Act requires licensing authorities to prepare and publish a licensing policy statement every three years. This order appointed 31 January 2007 as the first day of the initial three year period.
31 March 2006

Licensing Authority Policy Statement (England and Wales) Regulations 2006 SI 636
These regulations set out requirements as to the form and publication of a statement or a revision of a statement.
31 March 2006

REGULATIONS RELATING TO THE COMMENCEMENT OF THE 2005 ACT & TRANSITIONAL PROVISIONS

The Gambling Act 2005 (Commencement No.1) Order 2005 SI 2425
This Order simply brought s.355 of the Act into force, which allowed the making of further regulations, orders and rules.
28 August 2005

The Gambling Act 2005 (Commencement No. 2 and Transitional Provisions) Order 2005 SI 2455
This Order provided for the coming into force of a variety of sections of the Act, in two blocks. The first block relates to fundamental aspects of the Act such as the licensing objectives and the establishment of the Gambling Commission, and these came into force on October 2005. The second block relates to the appointed days that amendments to the English Licensing Act 2003 and Gaming Act 1968 would take effect, on either 24 or 25 November 2005.
Made 28 August 2005

The Gambling Act 2005 (Commencement No. 3) Order 2006 SI 631
This Order laid down the date that sections 166 (the ability for a licensing authority to "resolve" not to issue casino licences) and 349 (the three yearly statement of principles) would come into force as 31 March 2006.
Made 5 March 2006

The Gambling Act 2005 (Commencement No. 4) Order 2006 SI 2964
This Order specified that a number of provisions of the Act would come into force on 13 November 2006, including those sections which would enable licensing authorities to satisfy their duty to include details on family entertainment centres and prize gaming permits in the statement of principles.
Made 12 November 2006

The Gambling Act 2005 (Commencement No. 5) Order 2006 SI 3220
This order provided for the coming into force of Paragraph 23 to Schedule 7 of the Act on 5 December 2006, introducing a power for the Secretary of State to add, vary or remove details of relevant offences in Schedule 7 Part 1.
Made 4 December 2006

The Gambling Act 2005 (Commencement No. 6 and Transitional Provisions) Order 2006 SI 3272
This detailed Order provides for a number of sections of the Act to come into force in four blocks. The first of these concerns operating licences, personal licences, gaming machines and the Appeals Tribunal that came into force as of 1 January 2007. The second block concerns premises licences, FECs and AGCs (including FEC gaming permits), prize gaming permits, and inspections, and ordered that these would come into force on 30 April 2007. The third block concerns further provision for casinos, details regarding club premises and alcohol-licensed premises, and permits related to those types of premises, to come into force on 1 June 2007. The final block relates to all remaining aspects of the Act, to come into force on 1 September 2007, and provides for the repeal of The Betting, Gaming & Lotteries Act 1963, The Gaming Act 1968, and The Lotteries & Amusements Act 1976. The Order then lays down various and detailed transitional arrangements for existing operators holding

permissions under the previous legislation in order to "convert" their current permits and so on.
Made 6 December 2006

The Gambling Act 2005 (Commencement No. 6 and Transitional Provisions) (Amendment) (No. 2) Order 2007 SI 2169
This order makes a series of changes in order to allow further time for transitional purposes. For example amendments consequential on the provisions specifying the period for paying the first annual licence fee for club gaming and machine permits and alcohol-licensed premises gaming machine permits; and amendments relating to grandfathered premises licence applications.
16 August 2007

The Gambling Act 2005 (Commencement and Transitional Provisions) (Amendment) Order 2007 SI 1157
This order makes a series of changes in order to allow further time for transitional purposes. For example, it removed the reference to "two months" in relation to the last lodgement date for conversion applications by current Part II or III holders to Club Gaming Permits and Club Machine Permits, having the effect that the conversion application could be lodged at any time prior to the existing date of expiry. It also delayed the coming in to force of a number of provisions of the 2005 Act, presumably to allow local authorities more time to prepare.
29 April 2007

The Gambling Act 2005 (Commencement No. 7) Order 2007 SI 3155 (C. 127)
This Order specified that sections 214 to 234 of the 2005 Act, which relate to the provisions for Temporary Use Notices, would come into force on 1 December 2007.

Made 1 November 2007

The Gambling Act 2005 (Commencement No. 8) Order 2007 SI 1326 (C.59)
This Order specified that sections 7(5)(b)to(d),(6) and (7), 159 to 165, 175(2)to(8), 204 and Schedule 9 in relation to casinos would come into force on 20 May 2008.
Made 19 May 2008

REGULATIONS RELATING TO FEES

The Gambling (Premises Licence Fees) (England and Wales) Regulations 2007 SI 479
This regulation prescribes the annual fee and application fee for premises licences, along with the fees for associated items such as transfers, duplicates and so on.
21 May 2007

The Gambling Act 2005 (Personal Licence Fees) Regulations 2006 SI 3285
This regulation specifies the application, maintenance, variation and duplicate licence fees in relation to personal licences.
1 January 2007

Operating Licence and Single-Machine Permit Fees Regulations 2006 SI 3284
These regulations prescribe fees relating to operating licences (application, annual and other fees) and single-machine supply and maintenance permits (application fees only) issued under parts 5 and 10 of the Gambling Act.
1 January 2007 (Reg 27 1 September 2007)

Operating Licence And Single-Machine Permit Fees (Amendment) Regulations 2007 SI 269
These regulations amended the annual fees for non-remote operating licences.
1 March 2007

Operating Licence And Single-Machine Permit Fees (Amendment) (No.2) Regulations 2007 SI 1791
The regulations amended certain first annual fees and clarified others.
1 August 2007

Remote Gaming Duty Regulations 2007 SI 2192
The SI provided remote gaming duty's administrative rules. This included being registered by and making payments to HMRC.
1 September 2007

Gaming Duty (Amendment) Regulations 2008 SI 1949
This brought payments on account into line with new bands of gross gaming yield introduced by the Finance Act 2008.
1 October 2008

Operating Licence And Single-Machine Permit Fees (Amendment) Regulations 2008 SI 1803
The amendments create certain new fee categories and set new levels of fees that will be payable under the 2006 regulations from 1 August 2008.
1 August 2008

REGULATIONS RELATING TO PREMISES LICENCES

The Gambling Act 2005 Premises Licences (Review) Regulations 2007 SI 2258

This regulation provides for the procedure in relation to reviews of premises licences, including the notice period, the publication of the notice by the licensing authority, and the procedure when the notice requirements are not met correctly.
1 September 2007

The Gambling Act 2005 Premises Licences (Review) (Amendment) Regulations 2007 SI 574
The prior noted regulations (SSI 2007/394) erroneously made reference to licensing authorities giving notice of a review to "responsible authorities". Under s. 200(3)(a) of the 2005 however, only the licence holder is to be given notice. This amending regulation therefore removes references to the "responsible authorities" from the principal regulations.
7 January 2008

The Gambling Act 2005 (Premises Licences and Provisional Statements) Regulations 2007 SI 459
This highly detailed regulation makes a series of provisions in relation to premises licences under the 2005 Act, including the form and content of applications relating to premises licences ; the notice requirements in relation to premises licence applications ; the form and content of the licences themselves, and various other matters.
21 May 2007

The Gambling Act 2005 (Premises Licences and Provisional Statements) (Amendment) (England and Wales) Regulations 2007 SI 1775
This regulation makes some amendments to the principle regulations in relation to the detail required in plans, specifically for casino premises.
12 July 2007

The Gambling Act 2005 (Mandatory and Default Conditions) (England and Wales) Regulations 2007 SI 1409
This regulation prescribe conditions which shall apply generally to all premises licences, conditions that shall apply to a particular type of premises (e.g. casinos, betting, bingo etc), and conditions which shall apply to a particular type of licence in specified circumstances (e.g. a converted track premises licence in respect of horse-race courses).
21 May 2007

The Gambling Act 2005 (Proceedings Of Licensing Committees And Sub-Committees) (Premises Licences and Provisional Statements) (England and Wales) Regulations 2007 SI173
This regulation covers the conduct of licensing committees in relation to hearings under Part 8 of the gambling act. Such hearings may be held in relation to applications for a gambling premises licence, applications to vary, transfer or reinstate a gambling premises licence, for a provisional statement and for review of a gambling premises licence.
30 April 2007

REGULATIONS RELATING TO OPERATING AND PERSONAL LICENCES

The Gambling Act 2005 (Definition of Small-scale Operator) Regulations 2006 SI 3266
This regulation provides the definition of a "small scale operator" in relation to operating licences. The status affords certain exemptions in relation to the number of personal licences required to be held by people within the organisation.
1 January 2007.

The Gambling Act 2005 (Operating Licence Conditions) Regulations 2007 SI 2257

This regulation lays down conditions to be attached to operating licences, specifically in relation to the amounts that can be charged for participation and prize levels for bingo.

Made 25 July 2007

Personal Licences (Modification of Part 5 of The Gambling Act 2005) Regulations 2006 SI 3267

These regulations therefore specify a number of exclusion and modifications to part 5 of the Act, as it is to apply to personal licences.

1 January 2007

The Gambling Act 2005 (Relevant Offences) (Amendment) Order 2006 SI 3391

This regulation amends the list of relevant offences in respect of operating and personal licences under the 2005 Act, in particular by expanding on what may constitute a sexual offence.

8 January 2007

REGULATIONS RELATING TO LOTTERIES

The Small Society Lotteries (Registration of Non-Commercial Societies) Regulations 2007 SI 2328

This regulation provides the form and fee for registration of non-commercial societies, which is discussed in more detail in chapter 7 on lotteries earlier in this book.

1 September 2007

The Gambling (Lottery Machine Interval) Order 2007 SI 2495

This Order specifies that, in relation to s.235(2)(d)(ii) of the 2005 Act, if

a machine is provided which enables a person to purchase lottery tickets, there must be an interval of at least one hour between the time of entry to that lottery, and the time that the result of the lottery is announced.
29 August 2007

The Gambling Act 2005 (Incidental Non-Commercial Lotteries) Regulations 2007 SI 2040
This regulation prescribes the limits that lottery promoters may deduct in relation to paragraphs 4 and 5 of Schedule 11 to the 2005 Act. Promoters may deduct no more than £500 in respect of the costs of prizes; and £100 in respect of the costs of running the lottery.
1 September 2007

REGULATIONS RELATING TO TEMPORARY USE NOTICES

The Gambling Act 2005 (Temporary Use Notices) Regulations 2007 SI 3157
This regulation prescribes the activities which may be specified in a temporary use notice, the relevant fees, the form of the notice, and so on.
1 December 2007

REGULATIONS RELATING TO GAMING MACHINES

The Licensed Premises Gaming Machine Permits (England and Wales) Regulations 2007 SI 1833
This is the regulation which provides for the procedure dealing with applications for licensed premises gaming machine permits, i.e. where three or more machines are made available, and lay down the form of the application and the permit itself.
1 August 2007

The Gambling Act 2005 (Gaming Machines) (Definitions) Regulations 2007 SI 2082
This regulation provides definitions for "domestic computer" and "dual-use computer", as discussed in the chapter on Remote Gaming in this guide.
1 September 2007

The Categories of Gaming Machine Regulations 2007 SI 2158
This regulation lays down the categories of gaming machine under the 2005 Act as discussed in the relevant chapter above. They also provide for detail on when a person is considered to be using a gaming machine.
1 September 2007

The Gaming Machine (Single Apparatus) Regulations 2007 SI 2289
This interesting regulation provides for further guidance on the definition of "gaming machine" for the purpose of s.235 of the 2005 Act. The regulations state that a single piece of apparatus may be treated as more than one machine dependant on the number of people able to use it at one time ; and that each "player position" is to be treated as a single gaming machine.
1 September 2007

The Gaming Machine (Supply &c.) Regulations 2007 SI 2320
This regulations prevents the supply and installation of gaming machines which provide for the use of credit or debit cards.
1 September 2007

The Gaming Machine (Circumstances of Use) Regulations 2007 2319
This regulation provides information on a variety of technical issues do to with game play on machines, display of information on machines, the nature of prizes, payment limits and the "autoplay" feature some machines have.

Made 6 August 2007

The Gambling Act 2005 (Family Entertainment Centre Gaming Machine) (Permits) Regulations 2007 SI 454

This regulation provides for the form and fee for a family entertainment centre gaming machine permit, the renewal of same, and the fee for a change of name and duplicate copy, although with the exception of the fee for a change of name (£25), the remaining fees specified only relate to England & Wales.

21 May 2007

Gaming Machines in Alcohol-licensed Premises (notification fee) (England and Wales) Regulations 2007 SI 1832

the gambling act entitles persons who hold a relevant alcohol licence, to make available up to two gaming machines on the premises. to do so, licence holders must notify their licensing authority of their intention to rely on this entitlement and must pay a fee.

1 august 2007

REGULATIONS RELATING TO GAMING IN CLUBS

The gambling act 2005 (Club Gaming and Club Machine Permits) Regulations 2007 SI 1834

This is the regulation which deals with Club Gaming and Club Machine Permit application procedure, and lays down the form of the applications and the permits.

2 November 2007

The Gambling Act 2005 (Club Gaming and Club Machine Permits) (Amendment) Regulations 2007 SI 2689

These amending regulations substitute the application form contained in schedule 1 to the above regulation correcting an error and omissions in

the guidance notes on that form.
8 October 2007

The Gambling Act 2005 (Club Gaming Permits) (Authorised Gaming) Regulations 2007 SI 1945
This regulation provides for the types of games which may be played upon obtaining a Club Gaming Permit, and the appropriate participation fees.
1 September 2007

The Gambling Act 2005 (Gaming in Clubs) Regulations 2007 SI 1942
This regulation prescribes the forms of gambling which are permitted to be wholly or mainly the purpose of members' club or commercial club and extend to bridge and whist.
1 August 2007

The Gambling Act 2005 (Exempt Gaming in Clubs) Regulations 2007 SI 1944
This regulation prescribes the limits for "equal chance gaming" (i.e. poker) in club premises.
1 September 2007

REGULATIONS RELATING TO GAMING IN ALCOHOL-LICENSED PREMISES

The Gambling Act 2005 (Exempt Gaming in Alcohol-Licensed Premises) Regulations 2007 SI 1940
This is the regulation which prescribes the limits for "equal chance gaming" (e.g. poker) in alcohol-licensed premises.
1 September 2007

The Gambling Act 2005 (Exempt Gaming in Alcohol-Licensed Premises) (Amendment) Regulations 2007 SI 2240
This regulation deleted the erroneous reference to the non-existent paragraph 4 in the previous regulations.
1 September 2007.

The Gambling Act 2005 (Non-Commercial Equal-Chance Gaming) Regulations 2007 SI 2041
This regulation lays down the limits which must be observed in relation to non-commercial equal chance gaming. Participation fees may not exceed £8; the aggregate amount of prizes for the non-commercial event may not exceed £600; and where there is a series of events leading to a final, the aggregate amount of prizes in the final event may not exceed £900.
1 September 2007

REGULATIONS RELATING TO PRIZE GAMING

The Gambling Act 2005 (Limits on Prize Gaming) Regulations 2007 SI 1777
This regulation sets the limits that may be charged for participation in prize gaming, and the limits on the prizes which can be offered.
1 September 2007

The Gambling Act 2005 (Prize Gaming) (Permits) Regulations 2007 SI 455
This regulation lays down the fees and form of a prize gaming permit.
21 May 2007

REGULATIONS RELATING TO APPEALS

The Gambling Appeals Tribunal Fees Regulations 2006 SI 3287
This regulation sets the fee required for an appeal under s.141 of the Act. The fee level depends on the type of licence involved.
1 January 2007

The Gambling Appeals Tribunal Rules 2006 SI 3293
This regulation provides details on the procedure for appeals under the Act, from preliminary matters, the hearing itself as well as other general matters.
1 January 2007

The Gambling Appeals Tribunal (Amendment) Rules 2007 SI 577
This regulation was introduced to make a series of minor amendments to SI 3293
26 March 2007

ADVERTISING REGULATIONS

The Gambling Act 2005 (Advertising of Foreign Gambling) Regulations 2007 SI 2329
This regulation specifies the geographical areas to be treated as EEA states for the purposed of s.331(2) of the Act.
1 September 2007

The Gambling act 2005 (advertising of foreign gambling (amendment) regulations 2008 SI 19
These regulations amended the above regulation by adding Tasmania to the list of places that shall be treated as an EEA state but only in relation to remote gambling.
31 January 2008

INSPECTIONS

The Gambling Act 2005 (Inspection) (Provision of Information) Regulations 2007 SI 319

This regulation makes provision for the procedure in relation to the inspection of premises, whether by a police constable, gaming enforcement officer or other authorised person. Specifically, the person conducting the inspection must make sure the person to whom they make themselves known is an "appropriate recipient"; they must then inform that person that they may request a written record of the inspection. The regulations also specify what details should be included in any written record, if requested.

21 May 2007

INDEX